Busy Woman's COOKBOOK

by Sharon and Gene McFall

Third Printing – 2001
175,000 copies

Reprinted 2006

Copyright © 2000
Sharon McFall, Claremore, Oklahoma

ISBN: 1-930170-02-5

Additional copies may be ordered for $18.95, plus $3.50
shipping, (Texas residents add $1.89 sales tax per book).

Creative Ideas Publishing
7916 NW 23rd Street
P.M.B. 115
Bethany, OK 73008-5135

800-673-0786
Online ordering: *www.busywomanscookbook.com*

Printed in China

You may substitute light or fat-free ingredients in any recipe calling for milk, cream, butter or cheese to create a delicious low calorie dish.

Acknowledgements

We would like to express our appreciation to the good cooks in both our families — especially our mothers and grandmothers — who instilled in us an appreciation of good homecooked food.

Thanks to family and friends from all over the United States who have given us some of their favorite quick and easy recipes for inclusion in this book.

We also welcome the opportunity to honor the women in our stories who have accomplished so much.

Table of Contents

Foreword

The Pioneer Woman had no modern appliances, no electricity, no convenience store on the corner, no shopping center or discount super store. She delivered her children with no help — or if she was lucky — with the help of a midwife. She doctored her family, made most of their clothes, and cooked three meals a day on a range that heated the kitchen to stifling in the summer. She often had to help in the fields of the family farm. She worked from dawn to dusk.

She had it rough. Today's woman has a much easier lifestyle — right?

Today's woman may have a microwave, a freezer full of pre-packaged TV dinners and every available labor-saving appliance, but life is probably busier and more hectic than at any other time in history. She still doctors the minor ailments of her family; she does countless loads of laundry (at least one of her children will change clothes three times a day). In addition, she finds time for her children's dance classes, soccer practices, Little League games, and she often entertains to help her husband's business. In addition, she may be the head of a corporation; have her own business or shop; travel coast-to-coast; and has to contend with the rising problems in her community that directly affect her family such as drug use among young people; then, there's always watching CNN or CNBC to keep up with world affairs.

When does she find time to cook using all the wonderful appliances in her kitchen?

"Busy Woman's Cookbook" is for today's woman who must feed her family; is tired of eating out; is concerned about the nutritional needs of her family; and who really wants to be a little domestic without spending precious time in her kitchen. The 500 easy, delicious recipes in "Busy Woman" have a short list of ingredients (3 or 4) and require minimal time in the kitchen.

The lists of Famous First Women and the stories about women's accomplishments that are sprinkled throughout the book are not a complete list, nor a total compilation of women of note. The lists are in no particular order, but are included to entertain and inform. The stories and facts are meant to celebrate and showcase the accomplishments of women throughout history and from all over the world. These women have excelled in the face of great odds, in a male oriented society. If you have a story about a trailblazing woman, and would like to see her in future volumes, please let us know. We'd love to hear your stories and add them to our own.

About the Authors

Sharon McFall

Sharon is a native of Des Moines, Iowa. For the past 10 years she has traveled extensively in the United States and around the world. In her varied experiences she has coordinated major seminars in the Midwest for working women, owned and operated a restaurant and concessions at a major country music center, designed and developed gift shops and women's apparel shops in important tourist areas and was vice-president of operations for a dinner theatre.

She is the mother of four children and enjoys spoiling her two granddaughters and two grandsons. When not collecting recipes and writing cookbooks, Sharon promotes and books her husband, Gene McFall's one-man show, WITTY WORLD OF WILL ROGERS. She currently resides in Will Rogers' hometown of Claremore, Oklahoma.

Gene McFall

Around the globe and across the nation into 45 states, Gene McFall has performed his prize-winning role of Will Rogers since 1982. Other than James Whitmore, McFall was the first person to perform WILL ROGERS' USA. Drawing from the archives of the Will Rogers Memorial at Claremore, Oklahoma, Gene wrote his own one-man show, WITTY WORLD OF WILL ROGERS, in 1989. Cast as Will Rogers, he was a major player in the public television production, OKLAHOMA PASSAGE. In his classic Will Rogers' role, Gene McFall drew praise in performances before Will Rogers' own children, President George Bush, Supreme Court Justice Byron White, UN Ambassador Jean Kirkpatrick, scores of U. S. Senators and Congressmen, Governors and state lawmakers in stage productions and during shows at conventions. Gene is the radio and television spokesman for the Oklahoma Credit Union League.

In a special staff role, Gene keeps Will Rogers alive to the school children of Oklahoma in a special program sponsored by the Will Rogers Memorial Commission, the Will Rogers Heritage Trust, Inc. and the Oklahoma Legislature.

First
Impressions

beverages

spreads

dips

appetizers

Famous First Women

1. The first woman to have her name placed on the cornerstone of a U.S. government building was NELLIE TAYLOR ROSS, Director of the Mint. The building was the U.S. Depository in Fort Knox, Kentucky. No formal dedication ceremonies were held.

2. JULIE EVELINA SMITH of Glastonbury, Connecticut, in 1876 used her knowledge of Latin, Greek and Hebrew and made the first Bible translation by a woman.

3. HARRIET MAXWELL CONVERSE was the first white woman to become an American Indian chief in a ceremony by the Six Nations Tribe in New York on September 15, 1891. In 1884 she had been adopted as a member of the Seneca tribe in appreciation of her efforts on their behalf.

4. LADY ASTOR-NANCY WITCHER LANGHORNE was the first American born woman to become a member of Parliament in Great Britain. Representing the Plymouth constituency she took the oath on December 1, 1919, as a member of the House of Commons.

5. NAN JANE ASPINWALL left San Francisco, California, on September 1, 1910, with a letter from Mayor McCarthy to Mayor Gaynor of New York City. She delivered the letter on July 8, 1911, having covered 4,500 miles in 301 days, 108 of which were spent traveling. She thus became the first woman to make a solo trans-continental trip on horseback.

6. The first woman humorist, FRANCES MIRIAM BERRY WHITCHER, used the nom de plume "Frank" in 1846 in the Saturday Gazette. Her "Widow Bedottot" papers were re-published in book form in 1855 and sold over 100,000 copies.

PINK CLOUD FLOAT

1 (10 ounce) package frozen
   strawberries

1 cup milk

2 cups strawberry ice cream

Add strawberries, milk, and ice cream. Blend
until smooth. Makes 4 servings.

DOWN HOME FOLKS SPICE DRINK

2 quarts apple cider

2 teaspoons allspice

2 teaspoons whole cloves

4 sticks cinnamon

In a large pot combine apple cider, allspice,
whole cloves, and cinnamon sticks. Cover.
Cook slowly for 20 minutes. Remove cinnamon
sticks. Serve hot with lemon slices.

CREAMY CHOCOLATE SHAKE

2½ cups cold milk

4 teaspoons instant coffee powder

½ cup chocolate syrup

1 quart chocolate ice cream

Put 1 cup of cold milk, coffee, and syrup in
blender; spoon in ice cream. Blend smooth. Add
rest of milk; blend. Makes 6
servings.

DR. JAMES BARRY (1795–1865) *served forty years as an officer in the British Service at a rank equivalent to major general; fought a duel; received a regular medical diploma; acquired almost a celebrity status as a surgeon. Only upon "his" death was it discovered that he was a woman—the first woman doctor of the British Isles.*

CHOCOLATE SPLENDOR

1 medium banana

2 cups cold chocolate milk

¼ teaspoon vanilla

Peel banana; cut into 1 inch pieces. Wrap banana in foil; freeze solid. Place chocolate milk, frozen pieces of banana and vanilla in blender. Blend until bananas are pureed and well blended. Makes 3 servings.

PIZZAZZ PUNCH

2 (6 ounce) cans frozen limeade, thawed

3 cups cold water

2 (12 ounce) cans lemon-lime soda pop, chilled

½ pint lime sherbet

Mix thawed limeade in 3 cups of water. Mix. Just before serving, stir in soda pop. Pour into punch bowl. Float scoops of sherbet. Makes 8 servings.

SPARKLING CRANBERRY PUNCH

1 (6 ounce) can frozen pink lemonade, thawed

1 (32 ounce) bottle cranberry juice cocktail, chilled

2 (12 ounce) cans ginger ale, chilled

Prepare lemonade as directed on can in large pitcher. Stir in cranberry juice cocktail and enough ice to chill. Just before serving, stir in ginger ale. Makes 10 to 12 servings.

After being turned down by 28 medical schools, **ELIZABETH BLACKWELL** *was accepted by Geneva College in New York. The administration had left her admission up to a vote of the students, thinking they would reject her. As a joke, they voted unanimously to accept her. Their decision was final and she graduated at the head of her class in 1849—she became the first woman doctor of modern times.*

LIP SMACKER RUBY RED PUNCH

1 (6 ounce) can frozen lemonade, thawed

2 pints cranberry cocktail juice

2 (7 ounce) bottles ginger ale

In large pitcher, add lemonade, cranberry juice, and ginger ale. Chill and serve over ice. Makes 12 servings.

COOL OFF LEMONADE

1 cup sugar

5 cups cold water

6 lemons, juiced

Dissolve sugar in water. Add lemon juice and serve over ice.

APPLE HONEYED CIDER

3 cups apple juice

1 tablespoon sugar

¼ teaspoon cinnamon

⅛ teaspoon nutmeg

Put all ingredients in sauce pan. Heat until hot. Makes 4 servings.

SUSAN B. ANTHONY is the woman most closely identified with the American women's suffragette movement, and the ill-fated one dollar coin carried her likeness. In 1872 she led a group of women in Rochester, NY, to vote illegally in the national election to test the right to vote under the 14th Amendment. She was arrested, tried, and fined. She never lived to cast a legal ballot.

GABRIELLE "COCO" CHANEL, *one of France's most successful fashion designers, demonstrated with her clothes that casual could be elegant. Her Chanel No. 5 perfume became one of the best known fragrances in the world. After World War II she was arrested as a Nazi collaborator by the British, but was released after only three hours. She knew too much about other British high society collaborators.*

STRAWBERRY FROSTY

1 (4 serving) box strawberry-flavored gelatin

1 cup boiling water

1 quart cold milk

1 quart strawberry ice cream

Put strawberry gelatin and boiling water in blender. Blend at low speed until gelatin is dissolved. Pour ½ cup of gelatin mixture into measuring cup. Set aside. Add half the milk to remaining mixture in blender. Blend on low speed until mixed. Add half strawberry ice cream, blend until smooth. Pour into tall chilled glasses. Repeat with reserved gelatin, milk, and ice cream. Makes 6 servings.

SPECIAL TOUCH PUNCH

1 (48 ounce) bottle cranberry – mango drink, chilled

2 (25 ounce) bottles white grape juice, chilled

2 (16 ounce) bottles sparkling water

2 medium apricots, sliced

Mix cranberry-mango drink and grape juice in punch bowl. Just before serving, stir in sparkling water and apricots. Makes 16 servings.

OLD FASHIONED LEMONADE

1¼ cups sugar

½ cup boiling water

1½ cups fresh lemon juice

4½ cups cold water

Combine sugar and boiling water, stirring until sugar dissolved. Add lemon juice and cold water. Mix well. Chill. Serve over ice. Garnish with lemon slices, optional. Makes 8 servings.

TEETOTALERS COOLER

2 cups orange juice

1 cup lemon juice

4 cups apple cider

Combine orange juice, lemon juice, and apple cider in punch bowl. Add sugar. Stir until dissolved. Pour over ice cubes. Makes 7 servings.

SUNSHINE SLUSH

1 (12 ounce) can peach nectar

1 (6 ounce) can frozen orange juice

1 tablespoon lemon juice

3 cups crushed ice

Combine all ingredients in blender. Blend until combined. Makes 4 servings.

GOLDA MEIR *was born in Russia, but moved with her family to the United States when she was 8. In 1921 she and her husband moved to Palestine. When Israel was struggling for independence, she came to the U.S. and helped raise over 50 million dollars. She held numerous posts in the Israeli government and at age 70, in 1969, became the Prime Minister.*

CAPPUCCINO ICEE

²/₃ cup chocolate syrup, chilled

2 cups cold coffee

2 cups vanilla ice cream

1 tablespoon frozen whipped topping

Place syrup and coffee in blender. Cover and blend on high speed. Add ice cream, cover and blend until smooth. Serve over ice, top with whipped topping. Makes 6 – 6 ounce servings.

MOCHA COFFEE

½ cup instant cocoa mix

¼ cup instant coffee crystals

4 cups hot water

Combine cocoa and coffee crystals. Mix well. Add to hot water. Makes 4 servings.

HOLIDAY EGGNOG

4 eggs

8 tablespoons sugar

2 teaspoons vanilla

2 quarts cold milk

Separate egg yolks from whites. Beat yolks until thick. Add sugar, vanilla, and milk. Beat until thoroughly blended. Beat egg whites, then fold into mixture. Pour into tall glasses or cups. (Sprinkle with nutmeg) optional.

Early on the morning of September 6, 1870, **LOUISE ANN SWAIN,** *age 70, of Laramie, Wyoming, fastened a clean apron over her housedress and walked to the polls. She carried an empty pail for yeast to be purchased at a bakeshop on the way home. She voted and thus became the first woman in the world to cast a vote in a public election.*

MUCHO MARY

1 cup tomato juice

1 cup club soda

Slices of lime

Mix tomato juice and club soda. Pour into tall glasses over ice. Garnish with lime slices. Makes 2 servings.

WHIPPED HOT CHOCOLATE

4 cups milk

1 (4 ounce) bar sweet chocolate

$1/8$ teaspoon cinnamon

Heat milk and chocolate together until chocolate is melted. Stir in cinnamon. Whip until frothy. Serve warm. Makes 4 servings.

ORANGE TISSIE FREEZE

1 pint orange sherbet

2 cups orange juice

2 cups crushed ice

Combine orange sherbet, orange juice, and crushed ice in blender. Blend until thick and frosty. Garnish with orange slices, if desired. Makes 6 servings.

The **VIRGIN MARY,** *mother of Jesus, is without doubt the most famous woman of all times. Her fame and influence comes not from her life and work, but from the purposes she has served for Christians over the centuries. She has inspired poets, architects and painters, and has served as a spiritual intercessor for the Catholics of the world.*

ORANGE JUBILEE

2¼ cups milk

1 (6 ounce) can frozen orange juice

2 tablespoons sugar

½ teaspoon vanilla

Put milk, orange juice, sugar, and vanilla in blender. Blend until smooth. Add chipped ice. Makes 4 servings.

STRAWBERRY-BANANA SHAKE

1 cup cold milk

1 medium banana

1 pint strawberry ice cream

Put cold milk, banana, and ice cream in blender. Blend until smooth. Makes 3 or 4 servings.

AFTER DINNER DRINK

2 scoops chocolate ice cream

1 tablespoon coffee liqueur

1 cup cold coffee

Whipped cream

Put ice cream, coffee liqueur, and coffee in blender. Pulse on and off until mixture is slushy. Pour into 2 glasses and top with whipped cream. Makes 2 servings.

*One of America's most famous ladies, a gift from France in 1884, welcomes the world to New York Harbor—the **STATUE OF LIBERTY.** On her base a poem by EMMA LAZARUS states: . . . Give me your tired, your poor, your huddled masses yearning to breathe free, the wretched refuse of your teeming shore. Send these, the homeless, tempest-tossed to me, I lift my lamp beside the golden door.*

BUTTERMILK BLUSH

2 cups cold buttermilk

2 nectarines, chilled, peeled, and cut into pieces

¼ cup packed brown sugar

Combine all ingredients. Put in blender. Blend until nectarines are pureed. Serve in chilled glasses. Makes 4 servings.

CRANBERRY-ORANGE JIGGLER

1 (4 serving) box orange flavored gelatin

1 cup boiling water

2½ cups cranberry juice, chilled

4 orange slices

Dissolve gelatin in boiling water. Add cranberry juice. Pour over ice cubes in tall glasses and garnish with orange slices. Makes 4 servings.

LUSCIOUS PINEAPPLE SMOOTHIE

1 cup sour cream

1 (15 ounce) can sweetened condensed milk

2 cups milk

1 (16 ounce) can crushed pineapple

Combine sour cream, sweetened condensed milk, and milk. Freeze in a 2 quart ice cream freezer. Using 6 parts ice to 1 part salt, until partially frozen. Add pineapple, freeze firm. Remove dasher. Cover. Pack in ice and salt. Allow to ripen 1 hour. Makes 2 quarts.

JOAN OF ARC *was the most prominent female military leader in history. Her courage and faith inspired many literary works. She was captured in 1431 and turned over to the English who charged her with witchcraft and fraud. She was condemned on a technicality — disregarding an official order to put aside male dress during her imprisonment. She was burned at the stake. Her conviction was overturned by papal edict 25 years later. The French heroine was canonized as a Roman Catholic saint in 1920.*

FROSTY PUDDING MILK SHAKES

3 cups cold milk

1 (4 serving) box instant chocolate pudding

1½ cups vanilla ice cream

Pour milk into blender. Add pudding mix and ice cream. Cover and blend at high speed for 30 seconds or until smooth. Pour into glasses. Makes 4 to 6 servings.

MALTED MILK SHAKE

1 cup cold milk

¼ cup chocolate syrup

2 tablespoons malted milk powder

1 pint vanilla ice cream

Put cold milk, syrup, and malted milk in blender. Spoon in ice cream. Blend until mixture is smooth. Makes 3 servings.

HOT CRABMEAT SPREAD

1 (8 ounce) package cream cheese, softened

½ teaspoon horseradish

2 tablespoons grated onion

1 (7½ ounce) can crabmeat

Combine all ingredients. Mix well and put into 9 inch pie pan. Bake at 375 degrees for 15 minutes. Serve with crackers or rye rounds. Makes 8 servings.

ESTEE LAUDER, the daughter of poor Hungarian immigrants, worked her way up in the cosmetics industry by selling a face cream made by her uncle. She founded Estee Lauder, Inc., in 1946 and had great success with Youth Dew bath oil in the 1950's. She was named one of 100 women of achievement by Harper's Bazaar in 1967, and named one of the Top Ten outstanding Women in Business in 1970. She published her autobiography, Estee: A Success Story, *in 1985.*

PARTY BREAD SPREAD

2 (8 ounce) packages cream cheese

¼ cup sour cream

8 ounces dates, cut finely

Soften cheese at room temperature and blend at low speed for 1 minute. Moisten with sour cream gradually. Add dates. Makes 3 cups.

LOW-CAL CHEESE SPREAD

½ cup fat-free cottage cheese

¼ cup crushed pineapple, drained

1 teaspoon lemon juice

Combine cottage cheese, pineapple, and lemon juice. Mix well. Serve on cocktail rye bread or crackers.

SEASONED FRIED CHEESE

8 ounces Cheddar or Swiss cheese

¾ cup cornflake crumbs

½ teaspoon basil

2 eggs, beaten

Cut the cheese into 2½ x ½ x ½ inch sticks. Combine crumbs and basil. Dip cheese sticks into eggs, then roll in crumb mixture, coating evenly. Dip cheese into eggs and crumbs again. Chill to set the coating. In a heavy sauce pan or a deep fat fryer heat 2 inches of oil to 375 degrees. Fry cheese sticks a few at a time until golden brown. Drain. Keep warm in a 300 degree oven while frying the remainder. Serve warm with taco sauce.

INDIRA GANDHI was the world's first woman Prime Minister. She helped expand India's role as an international force and as a Third World voice. Her career was turbulent and contradictory in a young nation with many problems. When she was slain in 1984 by two of her Sikh bodyguards, rioting by Hindus took the lives of 2,733 Sikhs.

SHRIMP, CRAB SPREAD

1 (8 ounce) package cream cheese

1 (6 ounce) can crab meat, drained

1 (12 ounce) bottle cocktail sauce

1 (4½ ounce) can shrimp, drained

Mix cream cheese and crab. Mix well. Spread mixture on a serving plate. Spread cocktail sauce over mixture. Cover with shrimp and serve with crackers. Makes 8 servings.

10 CALORIE CHEESE SPREAD

½ cup cottage cheese

1 tablespoon instant non-fat dry milk

¼ teaspoon salt

1 tablespoon water

Combine all ingredients in blender. Blend until smooth. Spread on bread or crackers, or use as topping for baked potatoes. Makes ¾ cup.

SALMON CHEESE SPREAD

1 (7¾ ounce) can salmon

1 (8 ounce) package cream cheese, softened

2 tablespoons minced onion

¼ teaspoon liquid smoke flavoring

Drain salmon and flake, reserving 2 teaspoons liquid. Combine reserved liquid with salmon, cream cheese, onion, and liquid smoke, blend thoroughly. Chill. Makes 2 cups.

JUDITH A. RESNIC, an American astronaut, and **CHRISTA MCAULIFFE,** *a New Hampshire school teacher who had been chosen to be the first private citizen to fly in a space shuttle, were two of those who died on January 28, 1986, when the space shuttle Challenger blew apart 74 seconds after blastoff from Cape Kennedy, Florida.*

THREE ONION SPREAD

2 tablespoons olive or vegetable oil

3 large onions, chopped

1 tablespoon chopped parsley

8 ounces soft cream cheese with
  chives and onion

Heat oil in 10 inch skillet over medium heat.
Cook onions in oil about 5 minutes, stirring occasionally. Stir in parsley and cream cheese until smooth. Serve warm or cold with crackers.
Makes 12 servings. (use a red onion for color)

FRUITY CHEESE SPREAD

2 (8 ounce) packages cream cheese,
  softened

1 (4 serving) package gelatin, any flavor

¼ cup chopped pecans

Beat cream cheese and gelatin in large bowl
until well blended, add pecans. Cover and chill
for 1 hour. Serve with fruit, cookies, or crackers.

PICK-ME-UP DIP

1 (14½ ounce) can asparagus spears,
  drained

½ teaspoon dried dillweed

½ cup sour cream

¼ teaspoon hot sauce

Place all ingredients in blender. Whip until
smooth. Chill. Serve with chips. Makes 1 cup.

*Montana gave
women the right
to vote in 1914.
In 1916, four
years before the
19th Amendment
granted women
suffrage,*
**JEANETTE
RANKIN**
*became the first
woman ever
elected to
Congress. She was
a pacifist, and
along with 48
others voted
against the U.S.
declaring war on
Germany in
1917. In 1941 she
cast the only
"no", vote in the
U.S. Congress
against declaring
war on Japan and
entering World
War II.*

NO-TIME QUICK DIP

3 (6 ounce) rolls sharp process cheese

1 (10 ounce) can tomatoes and green chiles

1 king size package corn chips

In a bowl mash cheese (room temperature), tomatoes and chiles together. Put in pan on low heat until cheese melts. Serve warm with corn chips.

OVER NIGHT DIP

1 (10 ounce) package frozen spinach

2 cups mayonnaise

½ cup chopped green onion

½ cup finely chopped parsley

Cook spinach in well salted water until tender, drain thoroughly and mash. Mix and add other ingredients and let set 24 hours. Makes 3 cups.

TORTILLA DIP

1 pound hot sausage

1 (12 ounce) can evaporated milk

1 pound Velveeta® cheese

4 tablespoons picante sauce

Brown sausage and drain. Add all ingredients to pan. Heat until cheese is melted, and mixture is hot. Serve with tortillas.

MARIA ANN SMITH was in the 1860's growing various seedlings on her orchard near Sydney, Australia. She experimented with a hardy French crabapple from the cooler climate of Tasmania. From this she developed the late ripening "Granny Smith" apple. Because of its excellent keeping qualities it formed for many years the bulk of Australia's apple exports.

SHRIMP COCKTAIL DIP

1 (3 ounce) package cream cheese

1 teaspoon parsley

1 (4 ounce) jar shrimp cocktail

Place cheese in the center of serving plate. Sprinkle half of the parsley over cheese. Pour shrimp cocktail over cheese and sprinkle remaining parsley over top. Serve with crackers. Makes 4 servings.

HOT CHEESE ONION DIP

2 cups chopped onion

2 cups grated Swiss cheese

1 cup mayonnaise

Mix onions, cheese, and mayonnaise. Mix well. Place in oven safe bowl. Bake at 350 degrees for 30 minutes. Serve with crackers. Makes 3 cups.

NUTTY APPLE DIP

2 apples, peeled and grated

1 (8 ounce) package cream cheese

8 ounces dates

1 cup finely chopped pecans

In mixer or food processor, mix grated apples, cream cheese, dates, and pecans. Refrigerate until ready to use. Serve with graham crackers or ginger snaps. Makes 3½ cups.

MURASAKI SHIKIBU (c.978-1030) wrote what is regarded as the first great novel in world literature; The Tale of Genji. *This lady of the 11th century Japanese court produced a prose romance filled with believable characters in real situations.*

REFRIED BEAN DIP

1 cup refried beans

1 cup salsa

2 cups sour cream

In a saucepan combine all ingredients. Heat till warm. Serve with chips. Makes 4 cups.

MEXIE BEEF DIP

½ pound ground beef, cooked

1 (15 ounce) can no bean chili

8 ounces Mexican Velveeta® cheese

Put beef, chili and cheese in saucepan on low heat. Stir until cheese has melted. Serve with taco chips.

CHILE ZIP DIP

1 cup sour cream

1 (8 ounce) package cream cheese, softened

1 (12 ounce) bottle chile sauce

1½ tablespoons instant minced onion

Combine sour cream and cream cheese in bowl. Beat with mixer until smooth. Add chile sauce and onion; mix well. Makes 3½ cups.

BARBARA McCLINTOCK in 1983 became the first woman to win an unshared Nobel Prize in Physiology and Medicine. She was one of the most influential geneticists of the twentieth century. She never gave lectures and did not publish her findings for years.

NACHO DIP

1 pound ground beef

2 cups shredded Colby cheese

1 (16 ounce) can refried beans

1 (¼ ounce) packet taco seasoning

Combine all ingredients in saucepan. Cook on low heat, stir until cheese has melted. Makes 4 cups.

QUICK AND EASY PARTY SALSA

3 medium tomatoes, diced

1 small green chile, seeded and diced

¼ cup diced onion

⅛ teaspoon salt

In a bowl combine tomatoes, green chile, onion and salt. Mix well and chill. Makes 1 cup.

*The date of the first American patent issued to a woman, **MARY KIES,** for a weaving machine was May 5, 1809. Between the years 1815 and 1910, a total of 8,596 patents were granted to American women for inventions ranging from corsets and baby carriages to locomotive wheels and mining machines.*

BLACK BEAN SALSA

¼ cup chopped fresh cilantro

1 (15 ounce) can black beans, rinsed and drained

1 (9 ounce) package frozen whole kernel corn, cooked and drained

Combine all ingredients in medium bowl. Mix well. Cover and refrigerate, stirring occasionally, for at least 1 hour to blend flavors. Serve with tortilla chips. Makes 4 cups.

MEXICAN CHEESE DIP

8 ounces Mexican Velveeta® cheese

1 (15 ounce) can no bean chili

Combine cheese and chili in saucepan and cook on low heat. Stir until cheese has melted. Makes 3 cups.

CHILES CON QUESO

1 (16 ounce) jar cheese spread

1 (4 ounce) can chopped green chiles, drained

1 (2 ounce) jar diced pimientos, drained

Heat all ingredients over low heat, stirring constantly, until cheese is melted, about two minutes. Pour into fondue pot or chafing dish. Keep warm over low heat. Serve with tortilla chips or bite-size fresh vegetables. Makes 2⅓ cups.

MARGARET KNIGHT (1838-1914) encountered resentment, envy, cynicism, and contempt as a female inventor, but her persistence resulted in at least 27 inventions. However, at her death at age 76, her estate was appraised at only $275.05.

DYNAMITE DIP

2 cups sour cream

1 (1 ounce) packet beefy onion soup mix

2 to 3 tablespoons chopped jalapenos

Combine all ingredients, mix well. Makes 2 cups.

OLD WEST STYLE DIP

1 (8 ounce) package cream cheese, softened

1 (15 ounce) can no bean chili

3 tablespoons taco sauce

1 cup grated Cheddar cheese

Spread softened cream cheese on bottom of pie plate. Cover with chili, taco sauce and grated cheese. Bake 30 minutes at 300 degrees. Serve with tortilla chips.

ORANGE YOGURT DIP

1 (8 ounce) package cream cheese

6 ounces orange yogurt

½ cup orange marmalade

2 tablespoons chopped pecans

Beat cream cheese in medium bowl with mixer on medium speed until creamy. Beat in yogurt and marmalade until smooth. Spoon into serving bowl. Top with pecans. Makes 16 servings.

AMELIA EARHART *was the first woman to fly solo across the Atlantic and the first person to fly unaccompanied 2,400 miles across the Pacific from Hawaii to the U.S. mainland. Her disappearance during an around the world flight fueled many rumors—including her capture and execution by the Japanese just before the beginning of World War II.*

APRICOT DIP

1 cup sour cream

¾ cup apricot preserves

½ cup flaked coconut

⅓ cup finely chopped walnuts

Combine all ingredients, mixing thoroughly. Chill. Serve with melon balls. Makes 2 cups.

RHETT BUTLER ONION DIP

1 (1½ ounce) packet dehydrated onion soup

2 cups sour cream

1½ tablespoons Miracle Whip®

In bowl, mix onion soup, sour cream, and Miracle Whip®. Refrigerate several hours or overnight. Makes 2 cups.

PESTO DIP

1 cup sour cream

¼ cup basil pesto

1 medium tomato, diced

Mix sour cream and pesto until well blended. Add tomatoes on top of mixture. Serve with vegetables. Makes 10 servings.

CLARA BARTON, *a U.S. nurse, organized the first American chapter of the International Red Cross in 1881. During the Civil War, at the request of President Abraham Lincoln, she had compiled records for the identification of the war dead.*

FIESTA DIP

3 avocados, mashed

1 (8 ounce) package cream cheese

1 (8 ounce) jar picante sauce

1 cup grated Monterey Jack cheese

In serving dish, layer mashed avocados, cream cheese, and picante sauce. Sprinkle cheese over mixture. Chill. Serve with chips. Makes 6 to 8 servings.

CAESAR VEGGIE DIP

½ cup sour cream

¼ cup Miracle Whip®

¼ cup creamy Caesar dressing

2½ tablespoons shredded Parmesan cheese

Mix sour cream, Miracle Whip®, and Caesar dressing until smooth. Stir in cheese and cover. Refrigerate for 1 hour. Serve with vegetables. Makes 10 servings.

BAKED CRAB DIP

1 (6½ ounce) can crab meat

3 (8 ounce) packages cream cheese, softened

5 tablespoons milk

2 tablespoons Worcestershire sauce

Mix all ingredients and put into baking dish. Bake at 325 degrees for 15 minutes. Serve with crackers. Makes 8 servings.

MYRA BRADWELL *passed the Illinois Bar Exam with high honors in 1869 and was on her way to becoming one of America's first woman lawyers. Despite an appeal to the state Supreme Court, she was refused admission because of her gender. She was publisher and editor of* Chicago Legal News *and used its pages to advocate for women's rights, and for property ownership rights by women. She ran her own business under a special charter allowing a married woman to do so. In 1892 she was admitted to the Illinois Supreme Court and United States Supreme Court.*

SUSIE SHARP
was the first
woman appointed
a superior court
judge in the state
of North
Carolina. She
gained a
reputation for
being fair and
stern, and in
1974, after 12
years on the
North Carolina
State Supreme
Court, she
became the first
woman elected
chief justice of a
state supreme
court. Time
Magazine named
her one of
America's 12
most important
women. If
Senator Sam
Erwin (of
Watergate hearing
fame) had had his
way she might
have been the first
woman appointed
to the United
States Supreme
Court, but she
was ahead of her
time.

TEXAS DIP

1 (15 ounce) can chili without beans

1 (8 ounce) package cream cheese

½ cup jalapeno salsa

½ cup chopped black olives

Put chili and cream cheese in saucepan on low heat and cook until mixture is hot. Stir in salsa and black olives. Mix well. Serve with tortilla chips. Makes 8 servings.

GREEN CHILE DIP

1 (8 ounce) package cream cheese, softened

1 (4 ounce) can chopped green chiles

¼ teaspoon garlic salt

Mix cream cheese with chopped green chiles and garlic salt. Mix well. Makes 1½ cups.

PINTO BEANS GARLIC DIP

2 cups canned refried beans

¼ cup mayonnaise or Miracle Whip®

1 clove garlic, diced

1½ teaspoons ground red chiles

Mix all ingredients. Cover and refrigerate 1 hour. Serve with tortilla chips. Makes 2 cups.

GREEN ONION DIP

2 cups cottage cheese

1 cup sour cream

1 packet dry onion soup mix

4 green onions, finely chopped

Put all ingredients in blender. Blend on low speed until mixed. Pour into bowl and sprinkle with Parmesan cheese (optional). Chill and serve with green pepper strips.

GUACAMOLE DIP

8 ripe avocados

1/2 cup chopped green chiles

1 garlic clove, minced

1 teaspoon lemon juice

Peel and pit avocados. Mash avocados with a fork. Stir in remaining ingredients. Makes 2 cups.

DAB-A-DOO DIP

1 (4½ ounce) can deviled ham

¼ cup chopped scallions

1 cup sour cream

2 tablespoons horseradish

Combine all ingredients, mixing well. Chill. Makes 2 cups.

*The story of **TILLIE EHRLICH LEWIS** is a true "rags to riches" story. A broke 20 year old divorcee, her perseverance led her to make the San Joaquin Valley of California the nation's leading tomato producer. In 1978 the "Tomato Queen" was one of the ten highest ranking businesswomen in the United States.*

CHEDDAR PECAN ROLL

¼ cup sour cream

1½ cups grated Cheddar cheese

¼ cup chopped pecans

Combine sour cream and cheese in large mixer bowl. Beat at medium speed until well mixed. Stir in pecans. Shape mixture into 10 x 1¼ inch roll. Wrap in plastic food wrap. Refrigerate until firm (3 to 4 hours). To serve, slice into ¼ inch sections. Arrange on large platter with assorted fresh fruit, if desired. 40 appetizers

FRIED CHEESE BALLS

½ cup grated Cheddar cheese

½ cup bread crumbs

2 egg whites, whipped

½ teaspoon baking powder

Mix cheese, bread crumbs, egg whites, and baking powder. Mix well. Shape into 1 inch balls and deep fat fry at 390 degrees until golden brown. Serve with a dip.

In 1879
***BELVA ANN
LOCKWOOD***
*became the first
woman to practice
as a lawyer
before the
U.S. Supreme
Court. She had
drafted the law
allowing this,
which Congress
passed.*

HOT SAUSAGE BALLS

3 cups Bisquick®

1½ pounds hot pork sausage

4 cups grated Cheddar cheese

Mix Bisquick®, sausage and cheese. Shape into 1 inch balls and place on baking pan. Bake 20 to 25 minutes or until brown.

YUMMY CHEESE BALLS

2 cups buttermilk Bisquick®

½ cup grated sharp Cheddar cheese

⅔ cup milk

Mix all ingredients until soft dough forms. Drop dough by spoonfuls into greased muffin pans. Bake at 450 degrees 10 to 15 minutes. Makes 4 servings.

TUNA CHEESE BALL

2 (6 ounce) cans tuna, drained

1 (8 ounce) package cream cheese

1 tablespoon lemon juice

2 tablespoons grated onion

Mix all ingredients. Blend well. Chill. Shape into ball.

CHEDDAR CHEESE BALLS

1 pound pork sausage

3 cups Bisquick®

4 cups shredded Cheddar cheese

½ cup grated Parmesan cheese

Mix all ingredients. Shape mixture into 1 inch balls. Place into lightly greased 15½ x 10½ x 1 inch jelly roll pan . Bake at 350 degrees for 20 to 25 minutes. Serve warm. Dip in any kind of chile sauce.

ANNE S. PECK took up mountain climbing at age 35 and conquered heights never before scaled by man. In 1904 she became the first person to reach the top of Mount Sorata in Bolivia, climbing its 21,300 feet without oxygen.In 1908 she reached the greatest height attained on foot in the western hemisphere, Peru's Huscaran Mountain (21,812 feet).At age 61 she became the first climber of Mount Coropena in Peru, 21,250 feet.

BEEF CHEESE BALL

1 (8 ounce) package cream cheese

1 green onion, chopped

1 (3 ounce) package dried beef, chopped fine

1 tablespoon Worcestershire sauce

½ cup finely chopped pecans

Mix all ingredients, except pecans. Cover and chill. Shape into ball. Cover with pecans. Serve with crackers. Makes 6 servings.

DRIED-BEEF CANAPES

1 teaspoon minced onion

1 tablespoon butter or margarine

2½ ounces dried beef, finely chopped

1 (3 ounce) package cream cheese

Cook onion in butter until tender. Add dried beef and cook until beef is slightly crisp. Add beef mixture to cream cheese. Blend. Spread on assorted crackers.

QUEEN NOOR, born Lisa Halaby, was a cheerleader and member of the first coed class at Princeton University. She married King Hussein of Jordan in 1978. She has been very active in improving conditions for Jordanian women. She broke tradition by attending her husband's burial in 1999.

BLUE CHIPS NACHOS

1 (6 ounce) bag blue tortilla chips

2½ tablespoons chopped jalapenos

⅓ cup chopped black olives

1 cup grated Cheddar cheese

Put the tortilla chips in a 13 x 9 inch baking dish and spread them out evenly. Sprinkle the jalapenos, olives, and cheese evenly over the tortilla chips. Bake at 350 degrees for 10 to 15 minutes. Makes 2 servings.

DELIGHTFUL CANAPES

1 (2 ounce) can salmon, finely chopped

½ cup cream cheese

¾ teaspoon dried dill weed

2 large cucumbers cut into ¼ inch slices (24 slices)

Mix salmon, cream cheese, and dill weed. Spoon mixture onto each cucumber slice. Garnish with a cooked shrimp, if desired.

ANGELS ON HORSEBACK

8 fresh oysters

4 thin slices bacon

2 slices hot buttered toast, each cut into 4 squares

Simmer the oysters in their own liquid over low heat for 4 minutes. Drain and wrap each oyster in a half slice of bacon. Secure bacon with toothpicks. Place under hot broiler until bacon is crisp. Serve on squares of hot buttered toast.

SALSA BEEF NACHOS

½ pound ground beef

½ cup chunky style salsa

4 cups tortilla chips

1 cup shredded Mexican style cheese

Brown ground beef, drain. Stir in salsa; simmer 3 minutes. Arrange chips on microwave-safe plate. Top with meat mixture. Sprinkle with cheese. Microwave on high for 3 minutes. Makes 4 servings.

MARIE MONTESSORI (1870-1952) *was Italy's first woman physician. She worked with mentally retarded children and developed methods in education that continue today in Montessori schools in all parts of the world and influenced curriculums of nursery schools, kindergartens, and primary schools everywhere.*

BITE-SIZE NACHOS

1 (8 ounce) bag tortilla chips

1 (10 ounce) can jalapeno bean dip

1 (4 ounce) can chopped green chiles

½ pound Cheddar cheese, sliced thin

Place tortilla chips on cookie sheet. Put a dab of bean dip on each chip. Top with a dab of green chile, and end with a small slice of cheese. Bake at 350 degrees for 10-15 minutes. Serve hot. Makes 6 to 8 servings.

COOL MELON APPETIZERS

1 half cantaloupe

1 half honeydew melon

3 ounces thinly sliced fully cooked ham

ELIZABETH KENNY (1886–1952) was the first woman and the only person without a M.D. degree to receive a Distinguished Service Gold Key from the American Congress of Physiotherapy. This Australian nurse pioneered treatment that helped many polio victims avoid paralysis.

Remove seeds from melons. Use a melon baller to scoop out the pulp. Cut ham into 1 inch strips. Wrap one strip of ham around each melon ball. Fasten with a toothpick. Makes 36.

PARTY CHEESE BISCUITS

2 sticks butter or margarine

1 cup sour cream

2 cups self-rising flour

2 cups grated Cheddar cheese

Melt butter and sour cream. Sift flour into mixture, blending well. Add cheese and mix well. Pour into four small muffin pans sprayed with vegetable oil spray. Bake at 400 degrees for 15 to 20 minutes. Makes 48 biscuits.

WATERCRESS PINWHEELS

1 unsliced loaf of white bread

1 cup chopped watercress

2 (3 ounce) packages of cream cheese, softened

Salt

Remove crust from bread and slice lengthwise in 3/8 inch thick slices. Combine watercress, cream cheese and a dash of salt. Spread about 1/4 inch of mixture on each bread slice. Roll, wrap in foil, and chill well. Slice 3/8 inch thick. Makes 24 appetizers.

SWEET-'N-SOUR WIENER BITES

1 (6 ounce) jar prepared mustard

1 (10 ounce) jar currant jelly

10 frankfurters

Mix mustard and jelly in chafing dish or double boiler. Slice frankfurters in bite-size pieces. Add to sauce and heat through. Makes 8 servings.

CHICKEN TENDERS

2 pounds chicken breast, skinless and boneless, cut into 2 inch strips

1/2 cup prepared mustard

2 cups crushed pretzels

Pour mustard into shallow bowl. Add chicken strips, turn to coat. Roll coated chicken in crushed pretzels. Place on baking sheet sprayed with cooking spray. Bake at 400 degrees for 5 to 8 minutes. Serve with extra mustard. Makes 6 servings.

In 1853 **ANTOINETTE BROWN BLACKWELL** *became the first woman officially ordained as a minister in the United States. She was ordained in a Congregationalist Church in South Butler, NY, but later joined the Unitarian Church.*

TEX-MEX CHICKEN WINGS

2½ pounds chicken wings, separated at joints, tips discarded

1 cup barbecue sauce

1 tablespoon chili powder

½ teaspoon garlic powder

Place chicken in 15 x 10 x 1 inch baking pan lined with foil. Bake at 450 degrees for 35 minutes. Drain grease. Mix barbecue sauce, chili powder, and garlic powder. Brush chicken wings with mixture. Bake an additional 10 minutes. Makes 4 servings.

PARTY TACO WINGS

2 tablespoons taco seasoning mix

2 tablespoons fine dry bread crumbs

8 chicken wings

½ cup milk

Combine seasoning mix and bread crumbs in plastic bag. Separate wings at joints. Dip chicken pieces in milk, and shake in bread crumbs to coat. Place chicken in shallow baking dish. Microwave on high level until chicken is done, about 14 minutes. Turn every 4 minutes. Makes 4 servings.

An all-around athlete, **MILDRED "BABE" DIDRICKSON ZAHARIAS,** *was named female athlete of the century. In the 1932 Olympics she shattered four world records. She tried golf as a gag set up by sportswriter Grantland Rice, then became the sports' top female—82 victories in professional and amateur tournaments. She was six times named Associated Press Woman Athlete of the Year.*

CHICKEN SALAD APPETIZERS

1 cup deli chicken salad spread

¼ cup sliced oil-packed sun-dried tomatoes, drained

2 medium cucumbers cut into ¼ inch slices

¼ cup chopped ripe olives

Mix chicken salad spread and tomatoes. Spoon 1 tablespoon chicken mixture on center of each cucumber. Top with olives. Makes 16 appetizers.

PUFF AND GOLDEN CANAPES

1 cup mayonnaise

1 cup Parmesan cheese

5 dozen, 1 inch white bread rounds

3 green onions, chopped

Mix mayonnaise and cheese. Put on top of bread rounds. Top with onions. Broil for 2 to 3 minutes. Makes 5 dozen.

SHRIMP PIZZAZZ BITES

24 large corn tortilla chips

¾ cup black bean dip

½ cup chunky style salsa

24 medium shrimp, cooked, peeled, and deveined

Top each tortilla chip with 1 teaspoon bean dip, ½ teaspoon salsa, and 1 shrimp. Place on cookie sheet. Broil 5 inches from heat for 2 to 3 minutes. Serve immediately. Makes 24 appetizers.

DOROTHY THOMPSON was the first woman to head a major American news bureau abroad, the Philadelphia Ledger's Berlin Bureau. Her syndicated column, "On the Record," reached a larger and more diversified segment of the American public than any other column of the 1930's.

HOT POTATO CHIPS

Potato chips

1 lime

¼ cup hot pepper sauce

Bottled steak sauce

Use enough potato chips to fill a two quart bowl. Sprinkle the chips lightly with lime juice, tossing gently. Sprinkle with hot pepper sauce and steak sauce to taste. Serve immediately. Makes 6 servings.

SWEET POTATO CHIPS

2 sweet potatoes

Oil

2 tablespoons sugar

2 tablespoons butter

Peel sweet potatoes and slice thin. Fry in deep oil. Sprinkle with butter and sugar. Makes 4 servings.

DEVILED EGGS

6 eggs, hard-cooked

⅛ teaspoon prepared mustard

3½ tablespoons Miracle Whip®

1 teaspoon sugar

Cut hard-cooked eggs in halves. Slip out yolks, mash with fork. Mix in rest of ingredients. Sprinkle with paprika (optional).

WU CHAO
(620-705?)
was China's only woman ruler and reigned for fifty years—a period of peace and prosperity.She is considered one of the strongest leaders in Chinese history.

CHEESY POTATO SKINS

4 large baking potatoes

3 tablespoons margarine or butter

1½ cups grated Cheddar cheese

¾ cup sour cream

Bake potatoes until tender. Let stand until cool enough to handle. Cut potatoes lengthwise into halves. Cut crosswise in half again. Scoop out pulp, leaving ¼ inch shells. Place potato shells on rack in broiler pan. Brush with butter. Sprinkle with cheese. Broil 5 inches from heat until cheese melts. Serve with sour cream. Makes 8 servings.

STUFFED OLIVES SURPRISE

¼ cup butter, softened

1 cup grated sharp Cheddar cheese

½ cup flour

36 stuffed green olives

Cream butter and cheese until blended. Add flour and mix well. Chill dough 20 minutes. Drain olives and dry. Shape small portion of dough around each olive. Place on cookie sheet. Bake at 375 degrees for 15 minutes. Serve hot or cold. Makes 3 dozen.

In 1969, **SHIRLEY CHISHOLM** *from Brooklyn, the first black woman in Congress, announced her intention to become the first black and female candidate for the presidency of the United States. In 1984 she founded the National Political Congress of Black Women.*

TOPSY TURVY NUT CRACKERS

12 graham crackers

1 cup chopped pecans

1 cup butter

⅓ cup sugar

Line a 12 x 17 inch jelly roll pan with aluminum foil. Break crackers into pieces along markings on crackers and place broken crackers in one tight layer on covered pan. Sprinkle chopped pecans over crackers. Set aside. Place butter and sugar in a saucepan, bring to a boil for 1 ½ minutes. Pour sugar mixture over graham crackers. Bake at 275 degrees for 20 minutes. Cool and break.

PIZZA NIBBLERS

4 saltine crackers

3 teaspoons pizza sauce

1 slice mozzarella cheese, quartered

4 slices pepperoni

Spread one side of each cracker with pizza sauce. Top each cracker with a piece of cheese and a slice of pepperoni. Arrange crackers on a paper-towel lined plate. Microwave at 50% (medium) for 30 seconds. Makes 1 serving.

MARY KAY ASH

started in door-to-door sales for the Child Psychology Bookshelf and then Stanley Home Products. She took direct sales to a high level with her own company, Mary Kay Cosmetics which she founded in 1963.
The pink Cadillacs driven by her top sales people were great incentives and popularized her products.

BISCUIT NIBBLES

1 (10 count) can refrigerated biscuits

3 tablespoons butter, melted

½ cup grated Cheddar cheese

¼ cup chopped jalapeno peppers

Cut biscuits into quarters. Pour melted butter in 9-inch pie pan. Put biscuits in butter, coat each piece with melted butter. Sprinkle cheese and peppers on top. Bake at 350 degrees for 15 minutes. Makes 4 to 6 servings.

TURKEY PATE

2 cups cubed, cooked turkey or chicken

½ cup pesto

½ cup mayonnaise or Miracle Whip®

Place turkey, pesto, and mayonnaise in blender or food processor. Cover and process until smooth. Cover and refrigerate at least 2 hours. Makes 12 servings.

PECANS WITH-A-BITE

2 cups pecan halves

2 tablespoons margarine or butter, melted

1 tablespoon soy sauce

½ teaspoon ground cayenne pepper

Mix all ingredients. Spread pecan mixture in 15½ x 10½ x 1 inch jelly roll pan. Bake at 300 degrees for 10 minutes. Makes 8 servings.

JANE AUSTEN (1775-1817) is regarded as one of the greatest novelists of all time. Some critics claim she is the first great novelist. She was so modest that her name never appeared on the title page of her books in her lifetime-books such as Pride and Prejudice *and* Sense and Sensibility.

BACON-CRESCENT ROLLUPS

1 (8 count) package refrigerated crescent rolls

½ cup sour cream

Onion powder

12 slices bacon, crisp cooked, drained and crumbled

Unroll crescent rolls and separate triangles. Spread with sour cream; sprinkle with onion powder. Top with crumbled bacon. Cut each triangle into 2 equal wedges. Roll up. Place rollups on greased baking sheet. Bake at 375 degrees until golden brown—12 to 15 minutes. Makes 24.

First Lady **DOLLY MADISON** *was one of our nation's capital's most memorable hostesses. Even after her husband James Madison's death, she continued as an important figure in Washington. At age 61 she returned to Washington and established herself in Washington society where she reigned for 20 more years and was honored by four more presidents. She struggled financially, but was helped by friends until Congress ·purchased her husband's papers, giving her a small income.*

Accessories

Famous
First Women

7. EVA SHAIN was the first woman to judge a heavyweight championship fight — the Muhammad Ali — Earnie Shaver prize fight on September 29, 1977, at Madison Square Garden. She scored it 9 rounds for Ali, 6 for Shaver.

8. GRACE F. KAERCHER of Ortonville, Minnesota was elected on November 7, 1922 as first woman clerk of a state supreme court in the U.S., and was the first woman elected to a state office in Minnesota. She was reelected four times.

9. The first female space traveler, Russian cosmonaut VALENTINA V. TERESHKOVA, made 48 orbits of the earth in 1963. The trip took 70 hours, 50 minutes.

10. MAGGIE MITCHELL WALKER was born in a white woman's kitchen where her mother had formerly been a slave, but she grew up to become the first woman bank director in America and one of the nation's most successful entrepreneurs.

11. On November 9, 1924, NELLIE TAYLOR ROSS was elected in Wyoming as the nation's first woman governor. MIRIAM "MA" FERGUSON of Texas was elected the same day, but was installed January 20, 1925.

12. When JERRY MOCK landed her single engine airplane in Columbus, Ohio, April 17, 1964, she became the first woman to fly around the world alone. She made 21 stops and flew 22,858 miles.

13. CYNTHIA NICHOLS of Canada was the first woman to complete a double crossing of the English Channel. Her swim in 1977 took 19 hours, 55 minutes and beat the previous record for a round trip by either sex by more than 10 hours.

14. On June 18, 1983, SALLY RIDE became the first American woman to travel in space aboard the space shuttle Challenger.

NAVY BEAN SOUP

2 pounds small white navy beans

1/2 pound ham hock

1 medium onion, chopped

1 1/2 teaspoons salt

Soak beans overnight in cold water. In the morning drain and cover with fresh water, bring to a boil. Add ham hock, onion, and salt. Simmer for 4 hours. Add water when necessary so beans will be soupy.

EGG DROP SOUP

1 (10 3/4 ounce) can chicken broth

1 soup can water

1 tablespoon chopped green onion

1 egg, slightly beaten

Combine all ingredients in saucepan. Heat to boiling, stirring occasionally. Makes 4 servings.

TOMATO SOUP SHAKE IT UP

1 (10 3/4 ounce) can condensed tomato soup

1 cup whole milk

1/4 teaspoon salt

1/2 teaspoon ground nutmeg

Egg (optional)

Combine all ingredients in a blender until smooth. Chill. Serve in chilled soup mugs. Makes 4 servings.

Although the People's Party did not win a majority of seats in the National Assembly, on December 1, 1988, **BENAZIR BHUTTO** *was named Prime Minister of Pakistan. She was the first woman leader of a modern Islamic nation.*

QUICK TOMATO CHILI SOUP

1 (11½ ounce) can condensed bean and
    bacon soup
1 (10¾ ounce) can condensed tomato
    soup
1 (10½ ounce) can no bean chili
1 soup can of water

Combine in a large saucepan and simmer for 10
minutes. Makes 5 or 6 servings.

CLAM BISQUE

1 (10¾ ounce) can condensed clam
    chowder
1 (10½ ounce) can condensed chicken
    gumbo
1 can half and half (measure in one of the
    empty soup cans)

Combine in a medium saucepan. Heat until
well blended. Makes 4 servings.

CHICKEN AND RICE SOUP — THE EASY WAY!

½ cup uncooked white rice
3 cups chicken broth
1 teaspoon salt

Cook rice in chicken broth until rice is tender.
Season to taste. Makes 4 servings.

*GWENDOLYN
BROOKS was
the first African-
American to win
a Pulitzer Prize
for poetry. In
1976 she became
the first black
woman inducted
into the National
Institute of Arts
and Letters.*

MAKE YOUR OWN CHICKEN NOODLE SOUP

8 ounces noodles

3 cups chicken broth (either dissolve chicken bouillon cubes in water to make broth or buy it in a can)

Cook noodles in chicken broth until noodles are tender. Season to taste. Makes 4 servings.

FRENCH ONION SOUP

5 cups sliced onions

¼ cup butter

6 cups beef bouillon

Brown onions lightly in butter. Add to bouillon. Cover and simmer for 30 minutes. Makes 6 servings.

ONION SOUP WITH MUSHROOMS

1 (10½ ounce) can onion soup

1 soup can water

¼ cup sliced canned water chestnuts, drained

1 (2 ounce) can sliced mushrooms, drained

Combine all ingredients in saucepan. Heat to boiling, stirring occasionally. Makes 4 servings.

HELEN GURLEY BROWN became the standard bearer for single women with the publication of her book, Sex and the Single Girl, *in 1962.She took over and changed the format of* Cosmopolitan *magazine and made it one of the most successful in the world. She wa inducted into the Publisher's Hall of Fame in 1988.*

HAM AND BEAN SOUP

1 pound brown beans

1 teaspoon salt

1 dried red pepper pod

1 cup ham chunks

Put beans in crock. Cover with water and soak overnight. Drain. Put in kettle and cover with clean water. Add salt and dried red pepper pod. Bring to a boil and then reduce heat and cook until done. After beans have cooked for an hour, add ham.

ENGLAND
CLAM CHOWDER

1 (11 ounce) can condensed vegetable soup

1½ cups tomato juice

1 (7½ ounce) can minced clams, with their juice

¼ teaspoon ground thyme

Combine all ingredients in a 2 quart glass bowl. Cover and microwave at power level high for 15 minutes. Stirring 3 times. Makes 3 servings.

MARIA ANNA DE CAMARGO (1710–1770) was a dancer who won fame for her performances at the Paris Opera.She is said to have been responsible for the shortening of the traditional ballet skirt, which allowed more complicated steps to be seen.She was also one of the first celebrities to lend her name to merchandising— shoes and wigs.

LAZY DAY POTATO SOUP

3 cups diced, uncooked potatoes

½ cup diced celery

½ cup diced onion

2 cups milk

In saucepan combine potatoes, celery, and onions. Cover with water and cook until tender. Drain. Add milk and heat until hot. Add salt and pepper. Makes 4 servings.

CHICKEN FOR LUNCH

1 (10 ounce) package frozen baby peas

2 cups cooked chicken, cut into ½ inch pieces

8 ounces American cheese, cut into ¼ inch pieces

½ cup mayonnaise

Thaw peas to room temperature. Mix chicken, cheese, mayonnaise, and peas. Serve on lettuce leaves. Makes 4 servings.

OUT TO SEA SALAD

1 (8 ounce) package artificial crab

½ cup Miracle Whip®

2 stalks celery, chopped

2½ tablespoons diced onion

Combine all ingredients. Serve on a bed of lettuce. Makes 4 servings.

MAUREEN "LITTLE MO" CONNOLLY *was the first woman and the second person to achieve the "grand slam" in tennis in 1953, the United States Lawn Tennis Association, the Australian, the French and British championships. She won the U.S. title three consecutive years, 1951– 53, and the Wimbledon singles 3 years in a row, 1952–54.*

YOGURT EGG SALAD

2 hard-cooked eggs, chopped

2 tablespoons plain yogurt

2 drops lemon juice

1/8 teaspoon mustard

Combine all ingredients and forkblend lightly. Chill. Serve on lettuce or in sandwiches. Makes 2 servings.

WHAT-A-DELITE CARROT SALAD

2 cups grated carrots

1/2 cup raisins

1 (8¾ ounce) can pineapple tidbits, drained

1/3 cup Miracle Whip®

Combine all ingredients. Mix well. Chill and serve on bed of lettuce. Makes 4 servings.

THIS IS TOO EASY COLESLAW

1 pound shredded cabbage

1 tablespoon finely chopped onion

1/2 cup – 1/3 cup mayonnaise

Sugar, salt and pepper to taste

Combine cabbage and onion in a bowl and mix well. Combine mayonnaise and seasonings in a separate bowl, whisk until sugar is dissolved. Pour over cabbage and mix well. Chill, covered for at least one hour before serving. Makes 6 servings.

ANNIE JUMP CANNON (1863-1941) an 1884 Wellesley graduate, was the first woman to receive an honorary doctorate from Oxford University (1925). A member of Harvard University's astronomy staff, she was personally responsible for the classification of over 225,000 stars brighter than 9th or 10th magnitude, and is one of the major contributors to astronomy in the 20th century.

CABBAGE AND GREEN PEPPER SLAW

Grate one head of green cabbage and one green pepper, or buy a package of shredded cabbage at the supermarket and shred a green pepper and add to the mix.

Dressing:

6 tablespoons mayonnaise

¼ cup vinegar

2 tablespoons sugar

1 egg, beaten

Place all dressing ingredients into a glass jar with a tight lid and shake until well mixed. Pour over cabbage/green pepper mix. Chill until ready to serve. You can also sprinkle a little paprika over the salad before serving, to add a little color.

PINEAPPLE COLESLAW

1 (16 ounce) can crushed pineapple, drained

2 cups shredded cabbage

2 apples, cored and diced

¾ cup Miracle Whip®

Combine all ingredients and mix well. Cover and refrigerate 1 hour. Makes 8 servings.

EDITH LOUISA CAVELL was an English nurse who in 1907 was the first matron of the Berkendael Medical Institute in Brussels.It became a Red Cross hospital in World War I. In August, 1915, she was arrested by the Germans and charged with having helped about 200 Allied soldiers escape to neutral Holland. She did not deny the charges, was tried by court martial and executed.

JACQUELINE COCHRAN

in 1935 was the first woman to fly in the Bendix Transcontinental Air Race.She set the transcontinental record of 10 hours, 28 minutes in 1938.She was named the International League of Aviators' outstanding world's pilot from 1937-50 and in 1953.She was the first woman to fly a bomber across the Atlantic in World War II; the first woman to fly faster than sound (1953); made the first landing and takeoff by a woman pilot from an aircraft carrier; and in 1964 flew faster than twice the speed of sound.

CUCUMBERS AND DILL DRESSING

3 medium cucumbers, cut into thin slices

Do not peel the cucumbers.

Dressing:

½ cup vinegar

1 cup sugar

¾ cup water

1 teaspoon dried dill weed

Whisk dressing ingredients in a small bowl (or shake in a jar). Place cucumber slices and dressing in a jar with a tight fitting lid and refrigerate overnight. An excellent quick side dish for brunch or lunch.

UP ALL NIGHT GREEN BEAN SALAD

2 cups cooked cut up green beans

3 tablespoons French dressing

2 tablespoons finely chopped onion

3 tablespoons Parmesan cheese

Marinate beans overnight in dressing with onion. Add cheese. Makes 4 servings.

MACARONI SALAD

1 cup macaroni, cooked

2 stalks celery, diced

2 green onions, chopped

¾ cup Miracle Whip®

Put cooked macaroni in bowl. Add celery, onions and Miracle Whip®, mix well. Chill. Makes 2 servings.

COLD PASTA SALAD

1 pound pasta, cooked and drained
(use tri-color pasta for a pretty salad)

½ cup chopped celery

½ cup chopped green pepper

Italian dressing

Parmesan cheese (optional)

Mix pasta, vegetables and dressing and chill overnight. Sprinkle with Parmesan before serving. Makes 8 servings.

PRIMAVERA PASTA SALAD

2 (7 ounce) packages tortellini

4-5 cups chopped fresh vegetables (pick them up at the supermarket produce counter)

⅔ cup sliced, pitted, ripe olives (or get a medium can and drain them)

Cook tortellini according to package directions, drain. In a large mixing bowl, combine tortellini, vegetables, and olives. Use your favorite bottled creamy garlic dressing, or creamy ranch. Makes 6 servings.

MARY CASSATT *is regarded as the greatest woman artist of the 19th century, and helped redefine modern art. She has been called the most significant American artist, male or female, of her generation. She lost her eyesight in later years and had to stop painting.*

PEA SALAD

1 (10 ounce) package frozen green peas, thawed

4 ounces American cheese, cubed

½ cup celery, chopped

½ cup Miracle Whip®

Combine all ingredients. Sprinkle with salt and pepper. Mix well. Chill. Serve on bed of lettuce.

In 1968, **JOAN GANZ COONEY** *founded the Children's Television Network, which in turn produced "Sesame Street" in 1969. The show became the premier public television program for children, drawing an audience numbering in the millions when it premiered on 190 stations. The show has won Emmy and Peabody awards for excellence and Cooney has been inducted into the Academy of Television Arts and Sciences Hall of Fame, 1989.*

PORK AND BEAN SALAD

This has been to many picnics!

1 (16 ounce) can pork and beans

3 tomatoes, peeled and quartered

1 bunch green onions, chopped

1 tablespoon mayonnaise

Mix all ingredients, chill if desired and serve.

BACKYARD BBQ GREEN SALAD

4 cups fresh spinach, torn

1 (16 ounce) can artichoke hearts, (drained, halved and chilled)

¼ cup sliced radishes

5-6 cups salad greens, torn

Toss all ingredients and mix with your favorite salad dressing. This makes a pretty salad for a backyard barbecue. Try a spicy bottled dressing to bring out the flavors.

BRIAN'S FAVORITE LETTUCE SALAD

1 (3½ ounce) can French fried onions

½ head lettuce, torn into pieces

5 cups Romaine lettuce, torn into bite sized pieces

⅓ Italian salad dressing

Heat the French fried onions in a 350 degree oven for a few minutes, until crisp. Toss lettuce with Italian dressing. Scatter warm onions on top. Serve immediately. Can also top with small cherry tomatoes. Makes 6 servings.

CHAMPION SPINACH SALAD

1 pound spinach torn into bite sized pieces

8 ounces fresh mushrooms, sliced

8 slices bacon, fried and crumbled

Mix spinach, mushrooms, and crumbled bacon in salad bowl. Serve with Italian or ranch salad dressing. Makes 4 servings.

PEACH WHIP DIP

1 cup frozen whipped topping

1 cup peach yogurt

½ cup finely chopped peaches

Mix whipped topping, yogurt, and chopped peaches in bowl. Chill. Serve with fresh fruit. Makes 2 cups.

DOROTHY ARZNER *was the first woman member of the Directors' Guild of America, and was a pioneer in many areas of the motion picture industry. The only woman movie director from 1930 to 1943, she was one of Hollywood's Top Ten Directors in the 1930's and 1940's.*

DIPPING FRUIT DIP

1 cup crushed macaroon cookies

1 cup sour cream

2 tablespoons firmly packed brown sugar

In bowl mix all ingredients. Serve with fruit. Dip fruit in lemon juice diluted with water to prevent browning. Makes 2 cups.

MICROWAVE APPLESAUCE

6 apples, peeled and quartered

¼ cup water

⅓ cup sugar

¼ teaspoon ground cinnamon

Place apples and water in a two quart microwave safe baking dish. Cover and cook on high for 6 to 8 minutes or until tender. In a food processor combine cooked apples, sugar, and cinnamon. Process until smooth. Makes 1 quart.

NIFTY FOR TWO APPLE SALAD

1 large cold apple, chopped

1 large celery stalk, chopped

¼ cup chopped pecans

¼ cup Miracle Whip®

In bowl add apple, celery, pecans and Miracle Whip®. Mix well.

MARGOT FONTEYN, *a British dancer, was generally considered the prima ballerina of the 20th century.She became the leading dancer of the Royal Ballet, and was especially noted for her partnership with dancer Rudolph Nureyev in the 1960's and 1970's.*

CRANBERRY SALAD SPECIAL

1 (16 ounce) can whole cranberry sauce

1 (8 ounce) can crushed pineapple, drained

1 banana, mashed

1 (12 ounce) tub frozen whipped topping

Mix cranberry sauce, pineapple, banana, and whipped topping. Place in container and freeze. Cut into squares before serving. Makes 6 servings.

WALDORF SALAD

2 cups chopped celery

1/3 cup chopped walnuts

2 cups chopped tart apples

3/4 cup mayonnaise

In bowl, add celery, walnuts, apples, and mayonnaise. Mix well. Serve on lettuce leaves. Makes 4 servings.

PEAR LUNCHEON SALAD

1 cup cottage cheese

1/4 cup raisins

2 tablespoons Miracle Whip®

1 (8 ounce) can juice packed pear halves, drained

Combine cottage cheese, raisins, and Miracle Whip®. Slice each pear half into quarters. Arrange cottage cheese mixture and pear slices on lettuce. Makes 2 servings.

After the death of her husband, lawyer William Dodge in 1858, **MARY DODGE** *turned to writing books for children. Her 1865 book,* Hans Brinker; or The Silver Skates *became a children's classic. From 1873 she was the editor of* St. Nicholas Magazine.

YOGURT FRUIT SALAD CUPS

2 cups orange yogurt

½ cup sugar

½ cup chopped pecans

2 cups pineapple tidbits, drained

Combine yogurt and sugar until blended. Fold in nuts and pineapple. Spoon into 8 muffin cups. Cover and place in freezer until firm. Remove from muffin cups and place on lettuce to serve. Makes 8 servings.

HOMEMADE FRUIT COCKTAIL

1 ripe banana, sliced

2 oranges, seeded and cut into chunks

1 (8 ounce) can pineapple chunks, undrained

4 teaspoons flaked coconut

Combine fruits and juice. Spoon into 4 stemmed glasses. Sprinkle with coconut.

RITA DOVE held the top position for a poet in this country, United States poet laureate, from 1993 to 1995. She was the youngest person and the first African-American to be chosen for this honor. She won a Pulitzer Prize for her poetry in 1987.

PASSION FRUIT CUP

1 (20 ounce) can bing cherries, drained

2 tablespoons cornstarch

2 tablespoons lemon juice

Stir juice drained from cherries into cornstarch. Add lemon juice. Cook over low heat until thickened, stirring occasionally. Pour cherries into a 1 quart baking dish. Pour thickened juice over fruit. Bake at 300 degrees for 20 minutes. Serve warm or chilled, plain or sprinkled with chopped nuts and coconut. Makes 5 servings.

OLD SOUTH FRIED PEACHES

2 large peaches, not too ripe

2 tablespoons butter

4 tablespoons sugar

Peel and halve peaches. Place peaches cut side down in a skillet of hot butter. When edges are nicely browned, turn halves up. Sprinkle half the sugar over top side and allow the other side to brown. Turn and sprinkle with rest of sugar. Cook until sugar caramelizes slightly, turning the peaches to coat.

KIWI STRAWBERRY SALAD

3 kiwi, peeled and sliced

1 avocado, peeled and sliced

12 strawberries, hulled and sliced

Leaf or bibb lettuce

Using individual salad plates, arrange fruits and avocado on lettuce leaves. Serve with Orange Dressing (see below) or try one of the many excellent bottled citrus dressings. A light, pretty salad. Makes 6 servings.

Orange Dressing:

⅓ cup olive oil

3 tablespoons orange juice (use fresh if you have it)

3 tablespoons raspberry vinegar

Salt and pepper to taste

Combine all ingredients in a glass jar, shake until well mixed. Chill a bit and pour over kiwi strawberry salad.

ELLA FITZGERALD (1918-1996), "The First Lady of Song" was discovered at the age of 16 during an amateur hour at Harlem's Apollo Theater, becoming one of the world's most celebrated jazz singers. She was mainly a solo performer, but did perform and record with Louis Armstrong, Duke Ellington, Count Basie, and Jazz at the Philharmonic. She was the first recipient of the Society of Singers lifetime achievement award, 1989, an award now called the "Ella" in her honor.

AVOCADO-CRANBERRY BOATS

1 can jellied or whole cranberry sauce

½ - ⅓ cup finely chopped celery

3 avocados, peeled and halved with pit removed

French dressing

½ cup finely chopped pecans (optional)

Mix cranberry sauce and celery and place a scoop in the center of each avocado half. Top with pecans and your favorite salad dressing. Can also be served on a bed of lettuce for a pretty presentation. Makes 6 servings.

ORANGE SHERBET AMBROSIA

3 large oranges, cut in half

1 pint orange sherbet

1 cup fresh strawberries, sprinkled with sugar

⅓ cup shredded or flaked coconut

Separate orange sections from shell, removing all white membranes. Set aside. Line each orange shell with a ½ inch layer of orange sherbet, leaving room for fruit. Freeze until firm. Remove from freezer and smooth out the surface of the sherbet. Fill shells with reserved orange slices, strawberries and coconut. Makes 6 small servings.

Her nearly 2,000 poems were largely unknown during her lifetime. Over 1,700 of **EMILY DICKINSON's** *poems were discovered after her death in 1886. Literary scholars view her as one of our greatest and most original poets. "Parting is all we know of heaven/and all we need of hell."*

LUNCHEON FRUIT SALAD

1 (20 ounce) can pineapple chunks, drained

2 (11 ounce) cans mandarin oranges, drained

1 cup miniature marshmallows

1/3 cup mayonnaise or Miracle Whip®

Mix all together. Serve on bed of lettuce. Makes 6 servings.

CRUNCHY RAISIN SALAD

6 cups grated carrots

2 cups chopped celery

1 cup raisins

1/3 cup mayonnaise or Miracle Whip®

Mix all ingredients and chill. Makes 8 servings.

APPLESAUCE ORANGE SALAD

2 cups applesauce

2 (4 serving) boxes cherry-flavored gelatin

1/2 cup orange juice

2 cups lemon-lime carbonated beverage

Heat applesauce and gelatin until gelatin is dissolved. Add orange juice and lemon-lime beverage. Pour into a 5 cup mold. Chill until set. Makes 6 servings.

CHRISTINE DAVIES (Mother Ross) left the inn she had inherited and went to Flanders in search of her husband who had been pressed into service in the army. There she enlisted as a private under a man's name and fought in several battles. She was united with her husband in 1706, but he was killed in battle in 1709. She then married another soldier who was killed the following year. In England she was presented to Queen Anne, returned to her home in Dublin, Ireland, and married another soldier. She died in the Pensioners Hospital for Old Soldiers in 1739.

BUTTERMILK SALAD

1 (20 ounce) can crushed pineapple, undrained

1 (8 serving) box apricot-flavored gelatin

2 cups buttermilk

1 (8 ounce) tub frozen whipped topping

Bring pineapple to a boil in a saucepan. Stir dry gelatin into pineapple and mix until dissolved. Chill until partially set. Stir in buttermilk. Chill again until partially set. Fold in whipped topping. Refrigerate until firm.

DELIGHTFUL PEAR SALAD

1 (15 ounce) can pears

1 (4 serving) box lemon-flavored gelatin

1 (8 ounce) package cream cheese

1 cup whipping cream, whipped

Drain pears, pour 1 cup of juice into saucepan and bring to a boil. Dissolve gelatin in juice. Chill until almost set. Put pears and cream cheese in blender and mix well. Add gelatin mixture and blend well. Fold in whipped cream and pour into mold and chill.

GEORGE ELIOT (Mary Ann Evans— 1819–1880) was first published under a man's name because of the scandal of living with editor George Henry Lewis without benefit of marriage.She was the first woman to incorporate major intellectual ideas into her fiction.Some of her works are Silas Marner, Middlemarch, *and* Daniel Deronda.

COOL ORANGE SALAD

1 (8 ounce) can crushed pineapple, drained

1 (4 serving) box orange-flavored gelatin

1 (12 ounce) carton small curd cottage cheese

1 (8 ounce) tub frozen whipped topping

Mix pineapple, gelatin, and cottage cheese. Mix well. Fold in whipped topping and chill. Makes 4 to 6 servings.

COKE® HITS THE SPOT SALAD

1 (8 serving) box lime-flavored gelatin

1 cup Coke®

1 (10 ounce) bottle maraschino cherries, drained and chopped

1 cup chopped pecans

Dissolve gelatin in one cup of hot water. Add Coke®, cherries, and pecans. Pour into serving dish. Chill until firm.

CRANBERRY ORANGE RELISH

1 pound raw cranberries

2 oranges

2 cups sugar

Wash and pick over cranberries. Wash and quarter oranges, leaving the peel on. Remove seeds. Put cranberries and oranges through food chopper. Put in bowl and add sugar to desired sweetness. Add a little lemon juice if you like. Chill.

KATHARINE HEPBURN's first stage appearances were failures and many of her early movies were box office flops. She went on to win three Oscars and to become the most distinguished, durable, and individualistic actress in film history.

CLASSIC STRAWBERRY BANANA MOLD

1 (4 serving) box strawberry-flavored gelatin

1 cup boiling water

1 (10 ounce) package frozen strawberries

2 large bananas

1/2 cup sour cream

Dissolve gelatin in water and stir in strawberries until thawed. Add a little more water. Add bananas. Pour half this mixture into 9 x 9 inch pan. Top evenly with sour cream (save a little sour cream for the top). Pour remaining gelatin mixture on top. Chill until firm and cut into squares . Top with small dollops of sour cream.

PEACH FLUFF SALAD

1 (8 ounce) can crushed pineapple

1 (4 serving) box peach-flavored gelatin

2 cups buttermilk

1 (8 ounce) tub frozen whipped topping

In a medium saucepan, heat pineapple until very hot, stirring constantly, but do not boil. Remove from heat; add dry gelatin. Add buttermilk and mix well. Chill until set. Remove from refrigerator and fold in whipped topping. Chill before serving.

BETTY FRIEDAN's book, The Feminine Mystique, *effectively began the women's' movement of the 1960's and 1970's. Her later focus has been on age discrimination, publishing* The Fountain of Age.

RASPBERRY–APPLESAUCE SALAD

1 cup applesauce

1 (4 serving) box raspberry-flavored gelatin

1 (10 ounce) package frozen raspberries, thawed

Sour cream

Heat applesauce just to a boil. Add gelatin and mix well. Stir in raspberries. Pour into a 9 inch mold. Chill until set. Serve with sour cream. Makes 6 servings

PLEASE THEM COCKTAIL SALAD

1 (17 ounce) can fruit cocktail, undrained

1 (4 serving) box strawberry-flavored gelatin

1 (3 ounce) package cream cheese, softened

1 (8 ounce) tub frozen whipped topping

Heat fruit cocktail with syrup. Add gelatin and heat to boiling point. Remove from heat. Add cream cheese and stir until it melts. Fold in whipped topping. Chill. Makes 6 servings

DORIS HUMPHREY one of the founders of modern dance, started dancing at age 8. She danced and choreographed for the Denishawn Company in Los Angles and founded the Humphrey Weidman School and company. She originated the Juilliard Dance Theatre in 1955. Disabled by arthritis she gave up dancing in 1944, but was the Limon Company's artistic director from 1946–58.

THIS AND THAT FRUIT RELISH

4 tart apples

2 oranges

2 cups cranberries

1 cup sugar

Core and quarter unpeeled apples. Seed and quarter unpeeled oranges. Combine all fruits and chop thoroughly. In a bowl combine chopped fruit and sugar. Mix well. Cover. Chill for one hour. Makes 3 cups.

HOMEMADE SWEET PICKLES

1½ quarts dill pickles

3 cups sugar

½ teaspoon celery seed

½ teaspoon mustard seed

Drain and rinse pickles. Pour pickles into a glass bowl and cover with sugar. Let mixture stand overnight. Drain syrup, put into broiler pan, and add celery seed and mustard seed. Bring to a boil and pour over dill slices. Cool and refrigerate.

POPPY SEED DRESSING

½ cup mayonnaise

2 tablespoons sugar

1 tablespoon poppy seed

1 tablespoon lemon juice

In a bowl combine all ingredients. Mix well. Cover and chill. Makes 1 cup.

VIRGINIA WOLFE is considered one of the most important English writers.She took the novel from surface realism to the deeper reaches of consciousness, and greatly influenced many novelists who followed.Her books centered not on plot, but on the inner, psychological world of her characters.In 1941, depressed over the outbreak of war, she committed suicide by drowning herself.

PRESTO PESTO SALAD DRESSING

2/3 cup mayonnaise or Miracle Whip®

2/3 cup prepared pesto sauce

1/2 cup milk

1/2 teaspoon pepper

In a small mixing bowl, combine all ingredients. Pour dressing over pasta salad and toss until combined. Makes 6 servings.

LEMON HONEY FRUIT DRESSING

1/3 cup undiluted frozen lemonade

1/3 cup honey

1/3 cup vegetable oil

1 teaspoon celery seed

Combine all ingredients. Beat until blended and smooth. Serve over fruit salads. Makes 1 cup.

LOW-FAT TARTAR SAUCE

1 cup plain low-fat yogurt

1 cup low-calorie mayonnaise

1/2 cup pickle relish

1 tablespoon prepared mustard

Combine all ingredients, mix well. Chill. Makes 2½ cups.

DOROTHY THOMPSON's syndicated column interpreting political events for women readers, "On The Record," had a readership of 7-8 million in the late 1930's and 1940's, and was in more than 150 newspapers. A column in "Ladies' Home Journal" and an NBC radio program made her a powerful figure in molding public opinion.

GLADYS AYLWARD left school at 14 to be a parlor maid, but she dreamed of being a missionary in China. In 1930 she left England and spent her entire life savings on a ticket to northern China. There, with a Scottish missionary, **JEANNIE LAWSON,** *they founded the famous Inn of the Sixth Happiness. From there in 1938 she led over 100 children across the mountains on foot to safety from the Japanese invasion of World War II. She spent 9 years with the Chinese Nationalists caring for the wounded.*

THOUSAND ISLAND DRESSING

1 cup Miracle Whip®

½ cup ketchup

2 tablespoons sweet relish

1 egg, hard-cooked and finely chopped

In bowl, combine all ingredients and chill. Makes 1½ cups.

YOGURT DRESSING

1 cup yogurt

2 tablespoons Miracle Whip®
   or mayonnaise

1 teaspoon sugar

Dash lemon juice

In a bowl combine all ingredients and mix well. Cover and chill. Makes 1¼ cups.

SO EASY BLUE CHEESE DRESSING

1 tablespoon lemon juice

1 cup Miracle Whip®

8 ounces blue cheese

Dash garlic salt

Using a mixer — blend all ingredients. Store covered in refrigerator. Also can use ½ cup sour cream and ½ cup Miracle Whip®.

Compliments
to the
Chef

beef   _____

pork _____

poultry _____

seafood _____

Famous
First Women

15. On March 12, 1993, JANET RENO of Florida became the first woman United States Attorney General, appointed by President Bill Clinton.

16. In 1929 JANET GAYNOR won the first Oscar for best actress in "Seventh Heaven", "Street Angel", and "Sunrise". It was the first and only time an actress won for multiple roles.

17. JEANETTE RANKIN was elected the first U.S. Congress woman in 1916, a Republican from Montana.

18. LUCRETIA BORI, a Spanish soprano noted for her beauty as well as her voice was the first singer ever to become director of the Metropolitan Opera in New York City.

19. In 1963, AUTHURINE LUCY bravely faced Governor George Wallace and a riotous mob as she became the first black student at the University of Alabama.

20. CLARA ADAMS in 1939 was the first woman to fly around the world. The time for the Pan Am Airways Clipper seaplane was 10 days, 19 hours, and 4 minutes.

21. In 1881 the first birth control clinic opened in Amsterdam under the direction of DR. ARLETTA JACOBS.

22. MOTHER FRANCIS XAVIER CABRINI became the first American citizen to be canonized, in a ceremony by Pope Pius XII in 1946.

23. For her poetry, GABRIELA MISTRAL became the first Latin American to win the Nobel Prize in Literature, the only Latin American so honored.

24. On June 3, 1972, SALLY J. PRIESAND became the first female rabbi in the United States when she became an assistant rabbi at the Stephen Wise Free Synagogue in New York City.

25. NAOMI UEMURA, a Japanese athlete traveling by dogsled reached the North Pole from Elsmere on May 1, 1978. She was the first person to ever make such a trip alone.

DELICIOUS ROAST AND GRAVY

2½ to 3 pound roast

½ cup flour

2 (10¾ ounce) cans cream of mushroom

1½ cans milk

Sprinkle roast with salt, dredge in flour. Brown on all sides in skillet, put roast in baking dish. In skillet add soup and milk. Simmer for 10 minutes and pour over roast. Cover with tin foil. Bake at 350 degrees for 3 to 3½ hours. Makes 6 to 8 servings.

BUFFALO-STYLE BURGERS

1 pound ground beef

½ cup sour cream

¼ cup dry bread crumbs

1 (1½ ounce) packet onion soup mix

Mix all ingredients. Shape mixture into 4 patties. Place patties on rack in broiler pan. Broil 3 inches from heat until desired doneness.

EASY POT ROAST

3 pounds roast

2 (⅞ ounce) packets brown gravy mix

1½ cups water

In crock pot put roast. Mix gravy mix and water and then pour over roast. Cook on high 6 to 8 hours. If frozen 8 to 10 hours. Can add potatoes 2 hours before roast is done. Makes 6 servings.

ELIZABETH FRITSCH, English potter, studied harp and piano before attending the Royal College of Art in 1968–71.She is considered one of the most talented contemporary potters and her vessels are regarded on equal terms with the important painters and sculptors of today.Her work is sometimes inspired by music using coiling spires and geometric patterns in colored slips with matte texture akin to ivory frescoes.

TASTY CLUB STEAKS

2 tablespoons butter

1 garlic clove

4 club steaks, 1 inch thick

Salt and pepper to taste

Melt butter in skillet and add garlic. Sprinkle steaks with pepper. Cook in butter for 6 minutes, turning once. Salt as soon as meat is done. Makes 4 servings.

ANGELINA GRIMKE and SARAH MOORE GRIMKE were daughters of an aristocratic slaveholding family in Charleston, SC. They became the first women to speak out publicly against slavery and to argue in print for legal and social emancipation of women. Their book, American Slavery As It Is: Testimony of a Thousand Witnesses, *(1839) was a major source for Harriet Beecher Stowe while writing* Uncle Tom's Cabin.

CHILI CHEESE BURGERS

1½ pounds ground beef

1 packet chili seasoning mix

1 cup grated Cheddar cheese

Combine all ingredients and shape into 6 patties. Grill over hot coals. Serve on hamburger buns.

GROUND BEEF CASSEROLE

4 potatoes

1 medium onion

1 (10¾ ounce) can tomato soup

1 pound ground beef, browned

Slice potatoes and onions into a casserole dish. Mix ⅓ cup of soup with hamburger and place on top of potatoes and onions. Put remaining soup over top. Cover and bake at 350 degrees for 1 to 1½ hours. Makes 4 servings.

HAMBURGER STROGANOFF

1 pound ground beef

1 medium onion, chopped

1 cup sour cream

1 (10¾ ounce) can cream of mushroom
    soup

Brown ground beef and onion. Drain excess fat
and add sour cream and soup. Simmer 20 to 25
minutes. Serve over egg noodles. Makes 6
servings.

BAKED BEEF BRISKET

1 (3 pound) beef brisket

1 tablespoon salt

3½ ounces liquid smoke

6 tablespoons water

Place brisket in pan. Sprinkle salt over beef.
Mix liquid smoke and water and then pour over
beef. Marinate overnight. Remove brisket from
marinade and wrap in doubled heavy-duty aluminum foil. Place in shallow baking pan. Bake
at 250 degrees for 6 hours. Makes 6 servings.

*BILLIE
HOLIDAY
(1915-1959) is
regarded as the
greatest jazz singer
ever recorded, and
took the vocalist
from being an
accompaniment to
being the main
attraction.Her
style influenced
many other singers
such as Lena
Horne and Frank
Sinatra.Unfortunately
much of her life
was plagued by
alcohol and drug
addiction.*

CORNED BEEF AND CABBAGE

4 pounds corned beef

6 whole pepper corns

1 bay leaf

1 large head cabbage

In large pan put corned beef, pepper corns, and bay leaf. Cover with boiling water and cover. Simmer 4 hours. Cut cabbage in wedges. Put on top of corned beef and simmer the last 15 minutes of cooking. Makes 8 servings.

NADINE GORDIMER is only the seventh woman in ninety years to win the Nobel Prize for Literature. A native of South Africa, many of her novels express strong opposition to the policy of apartheid and deal with the harsh reality of black and white relations in South Africa—such as The Living Days, *1954,* July's People, *1981, and* My Son's Story, *1990.*

OVEN CHUCK ROAST

2 tablespoons dry mustard

1½ teaspoons water

3 to 3½ pounds chuck roast

½ cup soy sauce

Blend mustard with water to make a paste. Cover and let stand 10 minutes. Place foil in shallow baking pan. Place meat on foil. Stir soy sauce into mustard mixture, blending until smooth. Pour mixture evenly over roast. Fold and seal foil to cover roast. Bake at 325 degrees for 3 hours.

TACO BURGERS

1½ pounds ground beef

½ packet taco seasoning

¼ cup ketchup

¼ cup milk

Mix all together and shape in 6 patties. Grill. Makes 6 servings.

ANYDAY ROAST

3 to 4 pound beef chuck roast

⅓ cup creamy horseradish

½ cup water

Brown meat well on all sides. Spread with horseradish. Add water, cover and cook slowly for about 3½ hours. Adding more water when necessary. Makes 6 to 8 servings.

OVER NOODLES BEEF STEW

3 pounds beef, cubed

1 (1 ounce) packet dry onion soup mix

2 (10¾ ounce) cans golden mushroom soup

¾ cup drinking sherry

Chop meat into bite size pieces. Mix with soup mix, mushroom soup and sherry. Pour into casserole dish. Cover. Cook at 300 degrees for 3½ hours. Serve over noodles. Makes 4 servings.

VEAL CHOPS

¼ cup flour

1 teaspoon salt

1½ pounds veal chops, ½ inch thick

4 tablespoons shortening

Blend flour and salt. Dredge veal chops in flour. Melt shortening in skillet. Add chops and brown on both sides. Reduce heat, add small amount of water; cover and simmer 45 minutes. Makes 4 servings.

EVA HESSE and her Jewish family emigrated from Germany to the U.S. in 1939.She was a sculptor and worked in a variety of unusual materials— rubber, plastic, string and polythene.She made hauntingly bizarre objects designed to rest on the floor or against a wall or even suspended from the ceiling.Her unconventional techniques and imaginative work exerted a strong influence on later sculptors.

OVEN-FRIED VEAL CUTLETS

1 egg, lightly beaten

1 tablespoon corn oil

6 tablespoons Italian seasoned bread crumbs

1 pound lean ground veal

Stir egg and oil together in shallow dish. Put bread crumbs in another dish. Shape meat into 4 patties. Dip patty in egg mixture, then in crumbs. Arrange veal patties in baking pan with cooking spray. Bake at 450 degrees for 12 minutes. Makes 4 servings.

VEAL BARBECUE

3 pounds veal shoulder

¾ cup ketchup

½ cup chopped onion

2 lemons, sliced

Put veal in roasting pan. Cover with ketchup, onion, and lemon. Bake at 350 degrees for 2½ to 3 hours. Makes 6 servings.

OVEN BAKE STEAK

2 pounds round steak

1 cup flour

1 teaspoon salt

½ cup water

Cut steak into serving size pieces. Roll in flour and salt. Brown in skillet with a little oil. When steak is browned put in baking pan. Add water and cover. Bake at 350 degrees for 1½ hours. Makes 4 servings.

Due largely to the efforts of **GRACE MURRAY HOPPER** *(1906–1992) computer technology made the great leap forward from the lab to the laptop. She developed the concept of automatic programming that led to the* COBOL *(Common Business Oriented Language) programming language.*

BEEF AND NOODLES

2 (10¾ ounce) cans cream of chicken soup

1½ cups milk

2 pounds stew meat

Combine soup and milk. Salt stew meat and brown meat. Add to soup mixture. Put in a baking dish. Bake at 325 degrees for 3 hours uncovered. Serve over cooked noodles. Makes 4 servings.

MINUTE STEAKS

4 minute steaks

½ cup flour

1½ teaspoons salt

4 tablespoons oil

Dredge steaks in flour mixed with salt. Brown in hot oil on both sides. Lower heat and cook 15 minutes. Makes 4 servings.

BAKED BRISKET

1 (7 pound) brisket

2 tablespoons garlic powder

1 (4 ounce) bottle liquid smoke

Meat tenderizer

Trim off all visible fat. Place brisket on a piece of heavy foil in a baking dish. Punch several holes on both sides of meat with a knife. Pour entire bottle of liquid smoke over brisket and sprinkle with meat tenderizer. Seal meat in foil tightly. Bake at 250 degrees 7 hours. Makes 12 servings.

*In 1955 a theatre in New York City was re-named in honor of **HELEN HAYES** to mark the fiftieth anniversary of her appearance on stage as a child actress. She had leading roles in a great variety of plays and also acted on the radio, on television and in the movies.*

CREAMY SWISS STEAK

2 pounds round steak, browned

2 (10¾ ounce) cans cream of mushroom soup

1¾ cans milk

Put browned steak in crock pot. Mix cream of mushroom soup and milk. Pour over meat and cover. Cook 8 to 10 hours on low (high 4 to 5 hours). Makes 6 servings.

TASTY BARBECUE RIBS

2½ to 3 pounds spareribs

1 onion, sliced

1 (16 ounce) bottle barbecue sauce

Sprinkle ribs with salt. Place ribs in broiler pan for 15 minutes to brown. Put sliced onion in crock pot. Slice ribs into serving pieces and put in crock pot. Pour in barbecue sauce. Cover and cook on low 8 to 10 hours (high 4 to 5 hours). Makes 4 to 6 servings.

CROCK POT SWISS STEAK

1½ pounds round steak, cut ¾ inch thick

2 tablespoons flour

1 stalk celery, chopped

1 (15 ounce) can tomato sauce

Cut round steak into serving pieces. Dredge meat in flour. Place in crock pot. Top with celery and cover with tomato sauce. Cover and cook on low 8 to 10 hours (high 4 to 5). Makes 6 servings.

MARY HARRIS JONES (1830-1930) *a labor leader, "Mother" Jones was called the greatest woman agitator of her time. For over 50 years she worked to publicize and promote the cause of male workers in the coal and steel industries, child laborers in textile mills, and women workers in Milwaukee beer breweries.*

T-BONE STEAK

4 (12 ounce) T-bone steaks

1 tablespoon garlic salt

1 teaspoon pepper

4 tablespoons margarine, melted

Sprinkle steak with garlic salt and pepper. Pour melted margarine over steak. Let set one hour. Broil 4 inches from heat or grill to desired doneness.

CHICKEN FRIED STEAK

1 egg, beaten

¼ cup milk

1 cup flour

1½ pounds round steak, tenderized

Mix egg and milk. Put flour in shallow pan. Cut round steak into serving sized pieces. Dredge steak in flour, then into egg mixture. Dip again in flour and place in skillet with hot oil. Brown on both sides. Lower heat, simmer until done. Salt and pepper optional.

FANNY BLANKERS-KOEN, a Dutch athlete, dominated women's events in the 1948 London Olympics. She won four gold medals: 100 meters, 200 meters, 80 meter hurdles, and the 4 x 100 meter relay.Primarily a sprinter, she also held world records for the high and long jumps. Achieving success at a relatively late age of 30, she captured the imagination of the sporting world as "the flying Dutch housewife."

LAST MINUTE BEEF TERIYAKI

1 pound beef sirloin steak, cut into thin strips

1 tablespoon oil

3 cups fresh or frozen stir-fry vegetables, thawed

¾ cup bottled teriyaki stir-fry sauce

Cook and stir beef in hot oil in skillet for 5 minutes. Add vegetables and sauce. Simmer on low for 4 minutes. Serve over rice. Makes 4 to 6 servings.

SWISS ROUND STEAK

1½ pounds round steak, cut into 1 inch strips

½ cup chopped onion

1 (15 ounce) can stewed tomatoes

2 green peppers, seeded and cut into strips

Brown meat in large skillet. Add onion, tomatoes, and green pepper. Cover and cook for 1 hour. Makes 4 servings.

MEXICAN PATTIES

1 pound lean ground beef

¼ cup flavored bread crumbs

1 tablespoon minced green onion

1 tablespoon salsa

Combine all ingredients. Mix well and shape into 4 patties. Cook as desired. Makes 4 servings.

JUANITA KREPS from North Carolina (a native Kentuckian) was named Secretary of Commerce by President Jimmy Carter in 1977. She was the first woman to be appointed to that position and the fourth woman in U.S. history to be named to a cabinet post.

MOCK SAUSAGE PATTIES

2 pounds lean ground beef

2 teaspoons salt

1 teaspoon poultry seasoning

Combine all ingredients. Mix. Shape into 16 patties. Fry in nonstick skillet or broil until done. Makes 16 patties.

OLD TIME MEAT LOAF

2 pounds ground beef

1 package saltine crackers, crushed

1 onion, chopped

2 cups ketchup

Combine beef, crackers, onion, and 1 cup ketchup and mix well. Shape into a loaf. Pour 1 cup ketchup over top of mixture and bake at 350 degrees for 1½ hours. Makes 6 servings.

PARTY BURGERS

3 pounds ground beef

2 tablespoons instant chopped onion

½ cup flat beer

2 teaspoons salt

Mix all ingredients, form into 10 patties and grill 4 inches from flame to desired doneness. Makes 10 servings.

FRIDA KAHLO (1907–1954) was considered one of Mexico's greatest artists. She began painting while recuperating from a school bus accident because she was bored in bed. She was the primary subject of her works. "I paint self-portraits because I am so often alone, because I am the person I know best."

TASTY PORK CHOPS

2 large onions

4 pork loin chops, ¾ inch thick

2 tablespoons brown sugar

2 tablespoons cider vinegar

Cut onions into thick slices. Put a little oil in skillet and over medium heat cook onions until tender, put aside. In the same skillet, add pork chops and cook 5 minutes on both sides. In saucepan add brown sugar and vinegar. Heat to boiling, pour over pork chops, and add onions. Cook 5 minutes. Makes 4 servings.

SKINNY-MINNY PORK CHOPS

6 breakfast pork chops

1 medium onion

1 (8 ounce) bottle fat-free Italian salad dressing

Spray skillet with cooking spray. Braise chops on both sides. Slice onion on top of chops, cover with salad dressing. Cook over low heat for 30 minutes. Makes 4 to 6 servings.

TEX-MEX PORK CHOPS

6 boneless pork loin chops

1½ cups salsa

1 (4 ounce) can diced green chiles

1 teaspoon salt

Brown chops in skillet with a little oil. Add remaining ingredients, cover, and simmer for 20 minutes. Makes 6 servings.

President Grant had to intervene to get **BELVA BENNETT LOCKWOOD** *her diploma from National University Law School. For three years she lobbied Congress to pass a bill to allow women counselors to plead before the nation's highest tribunal. In 1879 she became the first woman to practice law before the United States Supreme Court.*

HUNGARIAN PORK CHOPS

1 (5½ ounce) box au gratin potatoes

4 cups chopped cabbage

¼ cup pimiento

4 pork chops, browned

Prepare potatoes following directions on package, except use a 2 quart casserole dish and increase water to 2½ cups. Stir in cabbage and pimiento, then top with chops. Bake at 400 degrees for 50 to 60 minutes. Makes 4 servings.

PORK CHOP DINNER

3 medium pork chops

1 tablespoon oil

1 pound package Green Giant® Pasta Accents; garlic seasoning frozen vegetables with pasta

¼ cup water

In large skillet brown chops in oil. Add pasta with vegetables, add water. Cover and cook on medium heat for 12 minutes. Makes 3 servings.

PORK CHOPS WITH-A-TWIST

4 lean pork chops, 1 inch thick

4 thin onion slices

1 (16 ounce) can tomatoes

Brown chops well on both sides in lightly greased skillet. Top each chop with a slice of onion. Cover with tomatoes. Season with salt. Cover tightly. Bake at 350 degrees for 1½ hours. Makes 4 servings.

Called "America's Sweetheart," the 16 year old **MARY PICKFORD** *began her movie career in 1909. She became the first movie star and reigned for 20 years as the world's most beloved film actress. She was a silent film star but won an Oscar for her first talkie,* Coquette. *She retired from acting in 1933.*

PORK CHOPS WITH APPLES

6 pork chops

3 or 4 unpeeled apples, cored and sliced

¼ cup packed brown sugar

½ teaspoon cinnamon

Brown chops on all sides in skillet. Place apple slices in buttered baking dish. Sprinkle with sugar and cinnamon. Top with chops. Cover; bake at 400 degrees for 1½ hours. Makes 6 servings.

COCA-COLA® PORK CHOPS

2 tablespoons oil

6 pork chops

1 cup ketchup

1 cup Coca Cola®

In skillet add oil and brown pork chops on both sides. Add ketchup and Coca Cola®. Cook on low heat for 35 minutes. Makes 6 servings.

CROCK POT PORK CHOPS

6 lean pork chops

½ cup flour

1½ teaspoons dry mustard

1 (10¾ ounce) can chicken and rice soup

Dredge chops in mixture of flour and dry mustard. Brown chops in a large skillet. Place browned chops in a crock pot. Add can of soup. Cover and cook on low for 6 to 8 hours. Makes 6 servings.

CLARE BOOTH LUCE *was managing editor of* Vanity Fair, *in 1933–34, and wrote the play and movie,* The Women *in 1936.She served in the House of Representatives and was United States Ambassador to Italy.Her husband was Henry R. Luce, founder of* Time *magazine.*

PORK LOIN ROAST

3 pounds boneless pork loin roast

1 (16 ounce) can frozen orange juice

½ teaspoon ground ginger

¼ teaspoon garlic powder

Place pork on rack in open roasting pan. Bake at 325 degrees for 2 hours. Mix orange juice, ginger and garlic powder. Baste roast with mixture last 20 minutes of roasting. Makes 6 servings.

PORK ROAST WITH CHERRIES

1 (16 ounce) can cherry pie filling

½ cup raisins

2 tablespoons lemon juice

2 pounds pork loin

Mix pie filling, raisins, and lemon juice. Place pork loin in baking pan. Bake at 325 degrees for 1½ hours. Spoon mixture over roast. Bake 30 minutes more.

MARINATED PORK TENDERLOIN

½ cup soy sauce

¼ cup sugar

2 tablespoons ketchup

1 (2 to 3 pounds) pork tenderloin

Mix soy sauce, sugar, and ketchup. Pour over pork tenderloin. Marinate pork tenderloin overnight. Bake uncovered at 350 degrees for 1½ hours. Makes 4 to 6 servings.

BESSIE SMITH's first recording, "Downhearted Blues" sold 780,000 copies in six months in 1923. The "Queen of the Blues" helped transform the folk tradition of the blues into an American art form with worldwide impact. Her last record was the Depression-era "Nobody Knows You When You're Down and Out."

OVEN-FRIED COUNTRY HAM

8 slices country cured ham, ½ inch thick

1½ cups water

¼ cup black coffee

Place ham slices overlapping in a 15 x 10 x 2 inch roasting pan. Add ½ cup water and cover with lid. Bake at 325 degrees for 60 minutes and remove slices. Skim off excess fat. Loosen brown particles clinging to pan, add ¼ cup coffee. Add 1 cup water. Return to oven to reheat. Serve the red-eye gravy with ham slices. Makes 8 servings.

When she was growing up, **LAURA INGALLS WILDER's** *family lived on several farms on the midwestern prairies. When she was in her sixties her daughter suggested that she write down her childhood memories—of which she had almost total recall.* Little House In the Big Woods (1932) *was the first in a series that was an instant hit in the U.S. The television series,* "Little House on the Prairie," *was a hit not only in this country but abroad.*

HAM AND SWEET POTATOES CASSEROLE

1½ pounds sliced ham, cut into 6 serving pieces

3 medium sweet potatoes, pared

3 tablespoons brown sugar

1½ cups hot water

In a skillet brown ham in oil. Place ham in a large casserole. Slice sweet potatoes over it. Sprinkle with brown sugar. Add water to drippings in skillet. Heat and blend. Pour over sweet potatoes. Cover. Bake at 350 degrees for 45 minutes and baste after 20 minutes. Remove cover. Brown for 15 minutes. Makes 6 servings.

PORKY SURPRISE

4 cups cut-up cooked pork

1 large onion, sliced

2 cups barbecue sauce

Cook and stir pork and onion in a 3 quart saucepan over medium heat until onion is tender, about 10 minutes. Stir in barbecue sauce. Simmer 10 minutes. Serve over rice, spaghetti, or noodles. Makes 4 servings.

BARBECUED BABY BACK RIBS

2 pounds baby back ribs

2 cups barbecue sauce

1 (12 ounce) can cranberry-raspberry crushed fruit

Place ribs in ungreased rectangular 13 x 9 x 2 inch pan. Mix barbecue sauce and crushed fruit. Spoon over ribs. Cover. Bake at 375 degrees for 55 minutes. Uncover and bake 20 minutes. Makes 4 servings.

LICKING GOOD SPARERIBS

3 pounds spareribs

¾ cup packed brown sugar

½ cup pineapple juice

½ cup prepared mustard

Place ribs in baking dish. Combine remaining ingredients and pour over ribs. Cover; bake at 350 degrees, basting occasionally for 45 minutes. Uncover, and bake 35 minutes. Makes 4 to 6 servings.

VALENTINA, a Russian born fashion designer, was noted for her dashing personality and her turbans and flowing gowns.She opened her first shop in New York City, 1928, but became best known for dressing such stars of stage and screen as Judith Anderson, Lynn Fontaine, Gloria Swanson, and Katharine Hepburn.

BARBECUED SPARERIBS

4½ pounds back ribs

½ cup soy sauce

1½ tablespoons cornstarch

Barbecue sauce

Place ribs in a large kettle with a cover. Add 3 cups of water. Bring to a boil and cook 5 minutes. Remove ribs and drain well. Brush ribs with a mixture of soy sauce and cornstarch. Let set 30 minutes. Place ribs on grill, 3 inches from heat. Cook until tender, about 20 minutes. Every 2 or 3 minutes ribs should be turned and basted each time with barbecue sauce. Makes 6 servings.

SOBER-AS-A-JUDGE FRANKS

1 pound frankfurters

1 (12 ounce) can beer, at room temperature

½ cup finely chopped onion

Arrange frankfurters in a 2 quart glass casserole. Pour beer over frankfurters. Sprinkle on onions. Cover. Microwave on high level for 10 minutes. Let stand for 5 minutes covered, before serving. Makes 4 to 5 servings.

LOUISE NEVELSON

is recognized as one of the major sculptors of the 20th century. She struggled for three decades for recognition of her work constructed from odd pieces of wood, found objects, cast metal and other materials, covered with black, white or gold paint. Near the end of her life she received more public commissions than any other American sculptor.

SUNDAY MORNING SAUSAGE RING

2 pounds pork sausage

2 eggs, beaten

2 tablespoons butter

1½ cups bread crumbs

Lightly butter a 9 inch ring mold. Mix all ingredients well and pack into mold. Bake 20 minutes at 350 degrees; take from oven and pour off excess fat. Bake 20 minutes more. Turn onto a warm platter and fill with scrambled eggs. Makes 8 servings.

PINEAPPLE LAMBBURGERS

1 pound ground lamb

1 teaspoon salt

½ teaspoon pepper

1 cup crushed pineapple, undrained

Combine meat with salt and pepper. Shape into 4 patties. Spray skillet with cooking spray. Fry patties over medium heat until cooked through. Remove patty to warm plate. Add pineapple to skillet. Heat until hot and bubbling. Pour over lambburgers. Makes 4 servings.

BEATRIX POTTER *began her first book,* The Tale of Peter Rabbit, *as a letter. She wrote and illustrated more than twenty such books, which became classics. Her animals lived in a fantasy land but were depicted in a realistic and intelligent manner.*

WESTERN LAMB CHOPS

4 lamb chops, 1 inch thick

1 teaspoon salt

1 (12 ounce) jar thick salsa

Place lamb chops on rack in broiling pan. Sprinkle salt over chops, then spread with 1/3 of salsa. Broil 4 minutes, turn chops; spread with remaining salsa. Broil 8 minutes longer for medium-rare or until desired doneness. Makes 4 servings.

CAJUN CHICKEN STRIPS

6 chicken strips

2 teaspoons canola oil

2 teaspoons Cajun seasoning

Brush both sides of chicken with oil and sprinkle with Cajun seasoning. Grill 5 to 6 inches from heat turning until cooked through. About 4 minutes per side. Makes 2 to 3 servings.

CREAMY CHICKEN SUPREME

6 chicken breasts, boneless and skinless

1 (10¾ ounce) can cream of mushroom soup

1 (10¾ ounce) can cream of chicken soup

1¾ cups milk

Brown chicken breasts on both sides. Place in 9 x 13 inch baking dish. Pour mixed soup and milk over chicken breasts. Bake at 350 degrees for 1½ hours. Makes 6 servings.

QUEEN VICTORIA *became Queen of England at age 18 in 1837. During her reign of 64 years, the longest of any British monarch, she saw her country develop from an agrarian self-contained country to a modern industrial nation whose colonial empire encompassed the globe.*

STUFFING TOPPED CHICKEN BAKE

1 (6 ounce) package stuffing mix

4 boneless, skinless chicken breast halves

1 (10¾ ounce) can cream of mushroom soup

½ cup sour cream

Fix stuffing following directions on box. Set aside and place chicken breasts in 13 x 9 inch baking dish. Mix soup and sour cream. Pour over chicken. Spoon stuffing evenly over top. Bake at 375 degrees for 45 minutes. Makes 4 servings.

CHICKEN 'N NOODLES

2½ to 3½ pounds chicken

2 cups water

1 cup chicken broth

1 (8 ounce) package egg noodles

Place chicken in crock pot. Sprinkle with salt. Add water and chicken broth. Cover and cook on low 8 to 10 hours (high 4 to 5 hours). Remove chicken from broth. Turn crock pot on high and add noodles. Bone chicken and cut up meat. Stir chicken into noodles. Cover and cook 45 minutes, stirring occasionally.

QUEEN ELIZABETH II's coronation as Queen of the United Kingdom took place in Westminster Abbey on June 2, 1953, after the death of her father, King George VI. She married Phillip Mountbatten in 1947 and they have four children. She is an avid horsewoman and often visits Kentucky where she has interests in breeding thoroughbred horses.

SOUTHWEST CHICKEN

8 chicken breasts

1½ cups barbecue sauce

8 slices mozzarella cheese

1 (4 ounce) can diced tomatoes with green chiles

Place chicken breasts in baking dish. Cover each breast with barbecue sauce. Cover. Bake at 350 degrees for 1 hour. Take out of oven and put cheese on breast. Broil 1 to 2 minutes. Top with tomatoes with green chiles. Makes 8 servings.

CREAMY BAKED CHICKEN

4 chicken breasts

1 (10¾ ounce) can cream of chicken soup

1 (8 ounce) carton plain yogurt

1 cup crushed stuffing mix

Place chicken breasts in baking dish. Spread soup over chicken, then yogurt. Sprinkle stuffing over mixture. Bake at 350 degrees for 60 minutes. Makes 4 servings.

In partnership with Susan B. Anthony the eloquent **ELIZABETH CADY STANTON** *would take stage and do most of the oratory for the women's suffragette movement. After a speech, a married minister said, "The Apostle Paul recommends silence for women. Why don't you mind him?" She replied, "The Apostle Paul also recommends celibacy for clergymen. Why don't you mind him?"*

CHICKEN FRIED CHICKEN

1 cup flour

1 teaspoon salt

1/2 teaspoon pepper

2 1/2 to 3 pounds frying chicken, cut in pieces

Mix flour, salt, and pepper in paper bag. Shake 3 or 4 pieces of chicken at a time in bag to coat. Place chicken in skillet in 1 inch hot vegetable oil. Cover; cook 15 minutes over medium heat. Remove cover, reduce heat, and keep turning chicken until all pieces are browned, 20 to 25 minutes.

CHICKEN BAKED DELIGHT

1/3 cup plain bread crumbs

1 (4 ounce) packet buttermilk ranch salad dressing mix

1/3 cup light sour cream

4 chicken breast halves, boneless and skinless

In shallow dish, combine bread crumbs and salad dressing mix, mix well. Place sour cream in another dish. Dip chicken in sour cream, coating well. Roll in bread crumb mixture. Place chicken on sprayed cookie sheet. Bake at 375 degrees for 35 minutes or until chicken is fork-tender and juices run clear. Makes 4 servings.

SONJA HENIE incorporated some of her ballet training into maneuvers in figure skating. The Norwegian-born American skater won the world amateur championships from 1926-1935 and the Olympic gold medals in 1928, 1932, and 1936. She was successful as a professional ice skater, and in ten motion pictures from 1937–1945, she was one of the leading box office attractions.

GRILLED CHICKEN SAUCE

1 cup lemon juice

½ cup apple cider vinegar

¾ cup butter or margarine, melted

1 teaspoon salt

Whisk together lemon juice, vinegar, butter, and salt. Apply sauce liberally to chicken as you grill. Makes 2 cups.

ZESTY ITALIAN CHICKEN

6 chicken fillets

1 (8 ounce) bottle zesty Italian salad dressing

1 tablespoon garlic powder

Place chicken in baking dish. Pour dressing over chicken and sprinkle with garlic powder. Marinate 1 hour or overnight. Bake at 350 degrees for 35 minutes. Makes 6 servings.

CHEEZ-ITS® CHICKEN

4 chicken breasts, boneless and skinless

1 cup sour cream

3 cups Cheez-its®, crushed

1 cup margarine, melted

Dredge clean chicken in sour cream. Roll in Cheez-its® crumbs. Place in baking dish with melted margarine. Turn over so margarine is on both sides. Bake at 375 degrees for 40 minutes. Makes 4 servings.

ZORA NEALE HURSTON is acknowledged as one of the most important black writers of the 20th century, and her books are usually included in most college courses on African-American writing. In her later years her works were neglected and she lived in extreme poverty and was buried in an unmarked grave in Fort Pierce, Florida.

COMPANY COMING CHICKEN

8 chicken breasts, boneless and skinless

8 slices bacon

2 (10¾ ounce) cans cream of mushroom soup

½ cup sour cream

Wrap each chicken breast with a slice of bacon. Place in shallow baking dish. Mix mushroom soup with sour cream. Pour mixture over chicken. Bake at 300 degrees for 2 hours. Makes 8 servings.

ITALIAN STYLE CHICKEN

6 chicken breasts, boneless and skinless

1 (8 ounce) bottle Italian salad dressing

6 tablespoons butter

3 tablespoons lemon juice

Wash chicken breasts and place in baking dish. Coat each breast with salad dressing. Sprinkle with lemon juice. Place 1 tablespoon butter on each breast. Cover and bake at 300 degrees for 2 hours. Makes 6 servings.

DAME JOAH HAMILTON, a New Zealander born in Australia, was an active sportswoman and won golf and swimming championships up to 1935. She was studying at the Sydney Conservatory of Music when an arm injury forced her to give up the violin. She turned to singing and performed in Handel's Messiah in 1938 and made her operatic debut the next year in Vienna. From 1945 she sang leading roles in some 30 operas. Her Turandot recording was the first classical record to win a gold disc for sales over a million.

FLAKY NUT CHICKEN

½ cup dry-roasted peanuts

¾ cup corn flakes

4 chicken breast halves, boneless and skinless

¾ cup honey mustard

Place peanuts and corn flakes in blender. Blend until the mixture resembles crumbs. Pour into bowl. Coat each chicken breast with honey mustard and then roll in the crumbs. Place in a greased baking dish. Bake 400 degrees for 30 minutes. Makes 4 servings.

CHICKEN AND CHIPS

1 (10 ounce) bag potato chips

¼ cup butter

1½ teaspoons garlic salt

2 to 3 pound broiler fryer, cut in pieces

Crush potato chips finely. Melt butter in frying pan and add garlic salt. Roll chicken in seasoned butter, then in chips. Place chicken in oblong 13 x 9½ x 2 baking pan. Bake at 350 degrees for 1½ hours. Makes 4 servings.

MARJORIE JACKSON *was the first Australian woman athlete of undoubted world class. She came to prominence by beating Fanny Blankers-Koen twice after she had swept the Olympic sprints in 1948. She had a two year period in which she set 13 world sprinting records, and capped it by winning both Olympic sprints at Helsinki in 1952.*

SOUTHERN FRIED CHICKEN

3 pounds fryer chicken

1½ teaspoons salt

1 cup flour

¾ cup oil

Clean chicken and salt. Dredge chicken pieces in flour. Heat oil in skillet, put in chicken, brown on all sides. Turn heat on low. Cover and cook 35 minutes. Uncover and cook 5 minutes more on high heat. Keep turning. Makes 6 servings.

TACO FLAVORED CHICKEN

4 cups corn Chex® cereal, crushed

1 (1.5 ounce) packet taco seasoning mix

½ cup butter or margarine, melted

6 chicken breast halves, boneless and skinless

Pour crushed cereal and taco seasoning in pie pan. Mix well. Pour butter in shallow bowl. Dip chicken breast in butter then roll in crumb mixture. Place in baking pan. Mix any leftover crumbs and butter and sprinkle over chicken. Bake at 375 degrees for 35 to 45 minutes. Makes 6 servings.

ELIZABETH GURNEY FRY established a precedent of human treatment in penal institutions, that rehabilitation, not retribution, was the proper purpose of prisons. The "Angel of Prisons" also founded the first shelters for the homeless in England, organized libraries, and was the first woman to appear before a Parliamentary Committee.

SWEET AND SOUR CHICKEN

1 (8 ounce) bottle Russian salad dressing

1 packet dry onion soup

1 (10 ounce) jar apricot preserves

2 whole chickens, cut into serving size pieces

Combine salad dressing, onion soup mix, and preserves. Mix well. Place chicken in single layer in baking dish. Pour mixture over chicken. Bake at 350 degrees for 1½ hours. Baste occasionally. Serve with rice. Makes 8 to 10 servings.

PRETZEL BAKED CHICKEN

3 pounds chicken, cut up into portion sized pieces

2 eggs, beaten

½ cup milk

3 cups pretzels, finely chopped

Clean chicken, pat dry. Mix eggs and milk. Put chicken in mixture. Place pretzels in sack, put chicken in one piece at a time in sack and shake until coated. Place on greased flat baking pan. Bake at 300 degrees for 35 minutes. Makes 4 to 6 servings.

AMY JOHNSON *was the first woman pilot to solo from England to Australia and she set many other records. At the outbreak of World War II she enlisted in the auxiliary transport service and was killed in a crash into the Thames while on duty.*

SKILLET HONEY CHICKEN

2 tablespoons butter

2 tablespoons honey

4 to 6 chicken breasts, boneless and skinless

½ cup orange juice

Melt butter and honey in skillet. Add chicken to skillet. Brown chicken over medium heat, then turn to low heat. Add orange juice to skillet and cover. Cook 10 minutes, then remove cover. Cook until liquid reduces to a glaze. Makes 4 to 6 servings.

RUNNING LATE CHICKEN BAKE

1 broiler chicken, cut in half lengthwise

1 stick butter or margarine

1 packet dry onion soup mix

Place chicken halves on aluminum foil large enough to bring up over the top and wrap tightly. Cut butter ¼ inch slices and arrange them over the top of the chicken. Sprinkle with dry onion soup mix. Cover tightly with aluminum foil. Bake at 350 degrees for 55 minutes.

MARGARET THATCHER *was the first woman prime minister of Great Britain, the first woman to ever head a major western democracy, and was the second longest serving Prime Minister in Britain's history.*

NO PEEK BAKED CHICKEN

2 tablespoons oil

6 chicken breast halves, boneless and skinless

1 (10¾ ounce) can cream of mushroom soup

½ cup milk

In skillet, heat oil, add chicken, brown on both sides. Place chicken in baking dish. Mix soup and milk. Pour over chicken. Cover and bake at 350 degrees for 1½ hours. Makes 6 servings.

POLYNESIAN CHICKEN

2½ pounds chicken pieces, skinned

1 (14 ounce) can crushed pineapple, undrained

1 (12¾ ounce) jar peach preserves

Spray a baking pan with vegetable oil cooking spray. Arrange the chicken pieces in pan and spray them lightly. Bake uncovered at 400 degrees for 30 minutes. Turn chicken pieces and bake uncovered for 20 minutes. Drain and mix the pineapple with peach preserves. Pour over chicken and bake for 20 minutes. Makes 4 servings.

*In 1977 **JANET GUTHRIE** was the first woman driver to compete in the Indianapolis 500 auto racing classic. Her car developed mechanical problems and she dropped out after 27 laps. She also went on to drive in the NASCAR stock car circuit.*

CHICKEN IN MUSHROOM GRAVY

3 pounds chicken, cut up

¼ cup chicken broth

1 (10¾ ounce) can cream of mushroom soup

1 (4 ounce) can sliced mushrooms, drained

Place chicken pieces in crock pot. Sprinkle with salt. Pour chicken broth and soup over chicken, add mushrooms. Cover and cook on low 7 to 9 hours (high 3 to 4 hours). Makes 6 servings.

GLAZED CHICKEN BREASTS

½ cup apple butter

½ cup molasses

¾ teaspoon ground ginger

4 chicken breasts, boneless and skinless

In medium bowl, mix apple butter, molasses and ground ginger. Add chicken, toss to coat, cover; refrigerate for 30 minutes. Line broiler pan with aluminum foil; put chicken in pan. Broil 20 minutes, turning occasionally and brushing with mixture. Makes 4 servings.

ALTHEA GIBSON *was the first black tennis player to achieve success at the highest levels of the game. Tall and elegant, she won the French and Italian singles championships in 1956, and the British and American titles in 1957 and 1958. She won the professional singles title in 1960. She later appeared in films and played professional golf.*

DELICIOUS BAKED TURKEY

20 pound turkey

1½ cups butter, softened

1½ tablespoons salt

1 cup hot water

Clean and dry turkey. Put in roasting pan. Rub butter all over turkey. Sprinkle with salt. Pour hot water in roasting pan. Cover with heavy tin foil. Seal tight. Bake at 350 degrees for 4 hours. Take tin foil off. Pour turkey juice over turkey. Bake uncovered until deep golden brown.

BAKED QUAIL

3 tablespoons oil

1 quail

½ cup flour

1½ cups whipping cream

Heat oil in skillet, dredge quail with flour. Brown on all sides in hot oil. Pour off excess oil. Add cream. Cover and simmer until tender. Salt and pepper (optional).

BROILED SALMON STEAKS

6 (8 ounce) salmon steaks

¼ cup butter, melted

1½ teaspoons lemon pepper seasoning

Season fish by dipping both sides in melted butter and sprinkle with lemon pepper seasoning. Place fish on hot grill, 6 inches from heat. Broil 5 to 6 minutes on each side. Makes 6 servings.

*In 1744 **ELIZA LUCAS** produced the first successful crop of indigo in the American colonies on her father's plantation. She also devised a workable method of extracting the bright blue dye. It became the agricultural base of South Carolina's economy until the Revolution.*

MEXICAN-STYLE FISH

1 (16 ounce) package frozen halibut

2 tablespoons margarine or butter

1 (8 ounce) jar jalapeno salsa

1 (2.2 ounce) jar sliced olives, drained

Place frozen block of fish on a 20 x 12 inch piece of heavy duty aluminum foil: seal securely. Cook on ungreased cookie sheet. Bake 25 minutes at 350 degrees. Turn back foil; pour melted margarine over fish, top with salsa and olives. Cook uncovered 15 minutes. 5 servings.

SPICY SNAPPER

2 pounds snapper fillets

2/3 cup tomato juice

3 tablespoons vinegar

1 (3/8 ounce) packet French dressing mix

Place fish in a single layer in a shallow baking dish. Combine remaining ingredients; mix well. Pour over fish and cover. Refrigerate 30 minutes. Place fish on broiler pan. Broil 4 inches from heat for 5 minutes, turn, baste with leftover mixture. Broil 5 minutes more. Makes 8 servings.

JULIE MORGAN was the first woman admitted to the College of Engineering at the University of California at Berkeley, and the first woman admitted and to graduate from L'Ecole Nationale Superieure des Beaux-arts in Paris. In 1902, she was the first woman to get an architect's license in California. One of her best known works is the Hearst Castle, in San Simeon.

FLORIDA STYLE RED SNAPPER

1½ pounds red snapper fillets

1 teaspoon salt

1 teaspoon pepper

1½ teaspoons grated lemon rind

Put the fillets in a lightly buttered baking dish and sprinkle with salt and pepper. Distribute lemon rind on top. Bake at 400 degrees for 20 minutes. Makes 4 servings.

QUICK AND EASY PERCH

2 pounds perch fillets

2 tablespoons corn oil

2 tablespoons lemon juice

Paprika

Place fish on sprayed broiler pan. Combine oil and lemon juice. Brush mixture on fish. Broil 4 inches from heat for 8 to 10 minutes. Turn once and baste. Sprinkle with paprika. Makes 6 to 8 servings.

SOUTHERN FRIED FISH FILLET

1 cup cornmeal

Salt and pepper

4 fish fillets

2 eggs, beaten

In bowl, add cornmeal, salt, and pepper. Mix. Dip fillets into eggs and then into seasoned cornmeal. Pour cooking oil into fry pan at least ½ inch deep. Heat to smoking stage. Drop fish into oil. Brown on both sides. Makes 4 servings.

NATALIE WOOD became the first movie star to appear naked in a Hollywood feature film when she rose from the bathtub in 1961's Splendor in the Grass *and ran down the hall. The scene was not shown in theatres during the movie's general release.*

SEA BASS BROILED

2 pounds sea bass fillets

½ cup pineapple juice

¼ cup steak sauce

Place fish in single layer in shallow baking dish. Combine remaining ingredients and pour over fish. Refrigerate covered for 30 minutes, turning once. Remove fish, reserving mixture for basting. Place fish on a broiler pan sprayed with cooking spray. Broil 4 to 6 minutes. Turn carefully and brush with mixture. Broil 4 to 6 minutes more. Makes 8 servings.

OVEN-FRIED FISH

1 pound flounder

2 tablespoons mayonnaise

5 tablespoons fine dry bread crumbs

½ teaspoon paprika

Cut flounder into serving-size pieces. Coat with mayonnaise on both sides. Combine bread crumbs and paprika in a shallow dish. Press fish into crumb mixture to coat both sides. Place on nonstick baking sheet. Bake at 450 degrees for 15 minutes. Makes 4 servings.

QUICK TARTAR SAUCE

¾ cup mayonnaise

½ cup drained sweet pickle relish

2 teaspoons lemon juice

In a bowl mix all ingredients. Place in refrigerator until ready to serve. Makes 1¼ cups.

BERYL MARKHAM on September 4 and 5, 1936, became the first woman to fly the Atlantic Ocean solo from east to west. She was slightly injured. She spent much of her life in Kenya, big game hunting and breeding horses. Her memoirs, West With the Night, written in 1942, became a best seller in 1983.

SAUCY FISH FILLETS

2 pounds fish fillets

¼ cup tomato juice

¼ cup steak sauce

2 tablespoons Italian salad dressing

Cut fillets into serving-size pieces. Place in non-stick broiler pan sprayed with cooking spray. Combine remaining ingredients and spread half of mixture on fish. Broil 4 to 5 minutes. Turn fillets. Carefully spread with remaining basting sauce. Broil 5 minutes more. Makes 8 servings.

BAKED RED SNAPPER

1 stick butter

¼ cup finely chopped parsley

1 tablespoon lemon juice

2½ to 3 pounds red snapper

In a 10 inch round baking dish, combine butter, parsley, and lemon juice. Microwave uncovered, on high, until butter is melted. Stir to combine ingredients. Place snapper in baking dish, turning to coat both sides. Cover with wax paper. Microwave on high 13 to 15 minutes. Turn over fish after 5 minutes cooking time. Makes 4 servings.

ELLEN SWALLOW RICHARDS (1842–1911) was the first woman to attend a scientific college, earning a doctorate in chemistry at Massachusetts Institute of Technology, and the first woman to teach at M. I. T. She made a comprehensive study of the scientific basis of nutrition and created two new professions, dietetics and home economics.

BASS WITH PARMESAN

2 pounds bass fillets

1 cup nonfat sour cream

4 ounces grated Parmesan cheese

2 teaspoons sliced green onions

Cut fillets into serving-size portions. Arrange in a single layer on no-stick baking dish. Combine sour cream and onions and mix. Spread over fish. Sprinkle fish lightly with Parmesan. Bake at 350 degrees for 15 to 20 minutes or until fish is flaky. Makes 6 servings.

SALMON PATTIES

1 (14¾ ounce) can pink salmon

2 eggs

10 crackers, crushed

½ teaspoon salt

Put all ingredients in a bowl and mix well. Form into patties and fry in oil until brown. Makes 4 servings.

GOLDEN FRIED SHRIMP

1 cup flour

2 eggs, beaten

1 cup cracker meal

1 pound shrimp, peeled and deveined

In separate bowls put flour, eggs, and cracker meal. Hold shrimp by tail, 1 or 2 at a time; dip first into flour, then egg, then cracker meal. Fry in ½ inch hot oil until golden, turning once. Makes 3 to 4 servings.

MARY ROBINSON, *a leftist lawyer in 1990 was elected the first woman president of Ireland with 52.8 percent of the votes in a run-off election. She was opposed by both of the two largest Irish political parties. She had campaigned for legalizing both divorce and contraception.*

SAUTEED SHRIMP

2 pounds raw shrimp

4 tablespoons butter

2 teaspoons minced parsley

Lemon wedges

Shell and devein shrimp leaving the tails on. Melt the butter in a skillet and when it foams, add the shrimp. Cook over high heat turning the shrimp once or twice. Cook 5 minutes depending on size. Remove from heat, sprinkle with parsley and serve with lemon wedges. Makes 4 servings.

SHRIMP SCAMPI

4 tablespoons butter

1½ pounds raw shelled and deveined shrimp

3 garlic cloves, minced

½ cup chopped parsley

In a large skillet, melt butter over medium heat. Add shrimp and cook 3 minutes. Remove shrimp and sprinkle with salt and pepper. Add garlic and parsley to skillet and cook over low heat. Cook 1½ minutes. Pour over shrimp and serve at once. Makes 4 servings.

ANNA SEWELL, an *English novelist, was an invalid most of her life. She wrote "Black Beauty, The Autobiography of a Horse" in 1877 as a plea for more humane treatment of animals. It is probably the most famous fictional work ever written about horses. Years later it was made into a movie starring a young beauty, Elizabeth Taylor.*

OVEN FRENCH FRIED SCALLOPS

1 pound scallops

½ cup French salad dressing

½ cup bread crumbs

1 teaspoon paprika

Wash scallops and pat dry. Dip in dressing, then roll in bread crumbs. Sprinkle with paprika. Spread scallops on nonstick cookie sheet. Bake at 500 degrees for 8 to 10 minutes. Makes 4 servings.

FRIED SCALLOPS

1½ pounds scallops

1¼ cups bread crumbs

2 eggs, beaten

Oil

Rinse the scallops, shake off excess water, and roll in bread crumbs. Dip into the beaten eggs and again in the crumbs. Heat ½ inch oil in skillet. When oil is hot, put in the scallops. Do only a few at a time and fry until crumbs are nicely brown. Drain on paper towels. Sprinkle with salt. Makes 4 servings.

FRIED OYSTERS

1 pint oysters

1 egg, beaten

2 tablespoons water

1 cup bread crumbs

Wash and dry oysters. Mix egg and water. Dip oysters in egg mixture then in bread crumbs. Deep fat fry at 360 degrees. Makes 4 servings.

EMMA HART WILLARD *founded the first permanent educational institution for women in America, Emma Willard School in Troy, NY. She eliminated needlework, knitting and other ornamental arts from the curriculum and replaced them with zoology, anatomy, geometry, trigonometry, and other subjects, which were considered at that time to be beyond the grasp of female minds.*

BASTING BUTTER FOR FISH

¼ pound butter or margarine, melted

1 teaspoon lemon juice

1 teaspoon dry mustard

2 tablespoons chopped chives

Put melted butter in small bowl. Blend in lemon juice, dry mustard, and chives. Baste baked or broiled fish.

LEMON CREAMED BUTTER

¾ cup butter or margarine

½ teaspoon salt

⅛ teaspoon ground white pepper

1 to 2 teaspoons fresh lemon juice

Cream butter in a warm bowl until it has the consistency of mayonnaise. Stir in salt, pepper, and lemon juice. Mix well. Great on fish. Makes ¾ cup.

MAUD WATSON was the winner of the first women's singles tennis tournament at Wimbledon in 1884. **MARY SUTTON** *in 1904 was the first American to win the championship.*

Main
Attractions

Famous
First Women

26. The first person to swim the 89 miles between the Bahamas and the United States was DIANA NYAD in 1979. During her trip of 27 hours, 38 minutes, she was escorted by relays of other swimmers to keep jellyfish away from her.

27. MARJORIE SWANK MATTHEWS was the first woman bishop of a church in the United States. She was ordained a Methodist minister in 1965 and became the ranking Methodist in Wisconsin in 1980.

28. When she arrived back in Sydney on June 5, 1988, after of voyage of 189 days, KAY COTTEE of Australia became the first woman to sail around the world alone and non-stop. She sailed 23,000 miles in an easterly voyage in her 36 foot sloop, Blackmore's First Lady.

29. The first dictionary compiled by a woman was "The Language of Fashion" published by MARY BROOKS PICKEN in 1940 in New York City. It contained 8,000 terms and 600 illustrations relating to wearing apparel.

30. EMMA M. NUTT went to work for the Telephone Dispatch of Boston, Massachusetts on September 1, 1878, and became the first woman telephone operator. Previously all operators had been men.

31. MARGARET LEECH was the first woman in history to win two Pulitzer Prizes. She was awarded the 1941 Prize for "Reveille in Washington" and the 1959 Prize for "In the Days of McKinley".

32. LUCY BREWER concealed her sex and used an alias to become the first woman U.S. Marine. She served on board the U.S. Constitution in its battle with the Guerriere in 1812.

33. The first woman federal regulatory agency chairman was HELEN DELICH BENTLEY. She was sworn in as chairman of the Federal Maritime Commission on October 27, 1969.

FAVORITE BAKED ASPARAGUS

1½ pounds fresh asparagus
6 tablespoons virgin olive oil
½ cup grated Parmesan cheese

Clean asparagus; put in saucepan with 1 cup water. Simmer 8 minutes. Lay in buttered baking dish. Drizzle with olive oil and sprinkle with Parmesan cheese. Bake at 200 degrees for 7 minutes. Makes 4 servings.

CASHEW ASPARAGUS

2 tablespoons butter, divided
¼ cup salted cashew nuts
1 pound asparagus, rinsed and trimmed
4 tablespoons water

In a saucepan, add 1 tablespoon butter and nuts. Cook and stir over medium heat. Drain nuts on paper towels. Place asparagus and remaining butter in saucepan. Cook for 1 minute. Add water, cover and cook for 4 minutes. Pour into serving dish and sprinkle with nuts.

PHYLLIS WHEATLEY, who was born in Africa, was sold to John Wheatly of Boston who encouraged her writing. She became the first black poet in the NewWorld, published in 1770.

CREAMY ASPARAGUS

1 (10¾ ounce) can cream of asparagus soup

2 teaspoons milk

2 (10 ounce) packages frozen asparagus cuts

In medium saucepan mix soup and milk over medium heat. Heat to a boil, stirring occasionally. Add asparagus. Reduce heat to low. Cover and cook 10 minutes or until asparagus is tender, stirring occasionally. Makes 6 servings.

MAPLE GLAZE BEETS

1½ pounds fresh beets

1½ cups water

½ teaspoon salt

4 tablespoons butter

1 cup maple syrup

Scrape and slice beets into a frying pan. Combine beets with ½ teaspoon salt and 1½ cups water. Bring to a boil. Cover and cook for 10 minutes. Uncover and cook for 3 minutes longer. Add butter and syrup. Cook on low heat turning beets to coat for 15 or 20 minutes. Makes 6 servings.

Although she had no formal education, **CAROLINE HERSCHEL,** *a German astronomer, discovered at least five comets and three nebulae in her own right. She was of tremendous help to her brother, William, who discovered the planet Uranus and was appointed Britain's royal astronomer.*

OVEN BAKED CABBAGE

1 medium head of cabbage, shredded

1 (12 ounce) can evaporated milk

1 cup bread crumbs

½ cup butter

Place cabbage in shallow 4 quart casserole. Pour milk over cabbage. Sprinkle with bread crumbs and dot with butter. Cover and bake at 350 degrees for 30 minutes. Uncover and bake 5 minutes more. Makes 4 servings.

SKILLET CABBAGE

1 medium head of cabbage, shredded

¼ cup butter

¼ cup water

2 slices of bacon, uncooked

In skillet, put all ingredients. Mix well. Cook slowly until tender. Stir occasionally. Makes 4 servings.

ORANGE GLAZED CARROTS

1 pound carrots, peeled, sliced

1 cup orange juice

¼ cup butter, melted

1 tablespoon sugar

Combine all ingredients in a saucepan. Cover and simmer 15 minutes. Uncover and cook until liquid is absorbed. Makes 6 servings.

PATRICIA ROBERTS HARRIS recently had a U.S. Postal Service stamp issued in her honor. She was the first Black American woman named ambassador to a foreign country, served as delegate to the United Nations, Secretary of HUD, Secretary of Health, Education and Welfare, and Dean of Howard Law School.

GLAZED CARROT STICKS

6 large carrots

3 tablespoons butter or margarine

1 tablespoon brown sugar

2 tablespoons honey

Pare carrots and cut into sticks. Steam until tender. Melt butter in saucepan and add sugar and honey. Add carrots and cook over low heat until glazed. Makes 6 servings.

BAKED CORN DISH

2 (8 ounce) packages cream cheese

1 stick butter or margarine

1 (4 ounce) can chopped green chiles

4 (14¼ ounce) cans corn, drained

Melt cream cheese and butter in microwave until soft. Add chiles and corn. Mix well. Pour into baking dish. Bake at 325 degrees for 30 minutes.

ROASTING EAR OF CORN

12 roasting ears of corn

Hot water

1½ sticks of butter

Leave the husks on and bake at 300 degrees for 30 minutes. Remove husks and all the silk. Rinse in hot water. Serve with butter.

MARTHA GRAHAM founded the world famous Martha Graham Company of dancers and The Martha Graham School of Contemporary Dance. She choreographed over 190 ballets during her lifetime. More than three fourths of her performers went on to become choreographers and directors of dance companies.

BAKED CORN ON THE COB

4 ears frozen corn

4 teaspoons margarine or butter

1½ teaspoons salt

Defrost corn at room temperature. Place each ear on a sheet of heavy-duty foil. Spread ear with 1 teaspoon butter. Sprinkle with salt. Wrap each ear in foil and secure ends. Bake at 300 degrees for 20 minutes. Makes 4 servings

GREEN BEANS AMANDINE

1 tablespoon blanched almonds

1 pound fresh green beans or 10 ounce package frozen green beans, defrosted

¼ cup chicken broth

Spread almonds in skillet. Heat until almonds are toasted. Remove almonds; combine green beans and chicken broth in skillet. Simmer uncovered until beans are crisp and tender. Sprinkle with almonds. Makes 3 servings.

STEWED GREEN BEANS

2 slices bacon

2 (16 ounce) cans green beans

1 (16 ounce) can stewed tomatoes

1 medium onion, sliced

Fry bacon until crisp. Place green beans and tomatoes in large pot. Add onion and crumbled bacon. Bring to boil and cook until juice is reduced to half. Makes 6 servings.

MARGARET HIGGINS SANGER *recognized a need, coined a word, and started the American birth control movement. She was the first individual to openly disseminate contraceptive information. Due largely to her efforts, birth control in some form is legal and accepted in all the United States and in most lands.*

GARDEN FRESH GREEN BEANS

2 pounds string beans

½ pound salt pork

1 quart water

1 medium onion, sliced

Cut beans approximately 1½ inches in length. Cube and brown pork. Bring water to a boil. Add beans, salt pork and onion. Simmer on low 2 to 3 hours. Makes 6 servings.

STRING BEANS AND SHALLOTS

½ cup butter

¼ cup minced shallots

1 (16 ounce) package frozen string beans

½ cup chicken broth

Heat the butter in a large pan. Sauté shallots in butter until transparent, but not brown. Add beans and chicken broth. Toss to blend. Cook on low heat. Cook until liquid is reduced to a glaze. Makes 6 servings.

FRIED GREEN BEANS

3 pounds fresh pole beans

1½ tablespoons bacon drippings

1 cup water

½ teaspoon salt

Wash and snap beans. Add bacon drippings to large skillet, add beans and stir-fry for 10 minutes. Add water and salt. Cover and cook 20 minutes. Makes 6 servings.

The reigning monarch of all media is **OPRAH WINFREY.** *Her influence is such that when she plugs a book on her TV talk show it becomes a best seller. When she starts a new exercise program, thousands of women adopt her regime. In 1985 she received an Academy Award nomination for Best Supporting Actress for* The Color Purple. *With her many holdings and interests she is well on her way to becoming America's first black billionaire.*

CANADIAN STYLE GREEN BEANS

2 ounces Canadian bacon, diced

1 pound fresh green beans, chopped

1 small onion, chopped

¼ cup water

Fry bacon, stirring constantly until lightly browned. Combine green beans, onion, and water in saucepan. Add bacon. Cover and cook 12 to 15 minutes. Makes 6 servings.

CREAMED GREEN BEANS

2 teaspoons melted butter

2 teaspoons flour

1 cup milk

1 can whole string beans, drained

In a saucepan combine butter, flour, and milk. Cook slowly, stirring constantly until thickened. Place beans in a greased casserole. Cover with sauce. Bake at 350 degrees for 20 to 25 minutes. Makes 6 servings.

OVEN-COOKED BROCCOLI

1½ pounds fresh broccoli

1 tablespoon butter or margarine

½ teaspoon salt

Wash broccoli. Spread in a buttered baking dish. Add salt and cover. Bake at 350 degrees for 15 minutes. Makes 6 servings.

CALAMITY JANE (Martha Jane Canary) was a rough, tough frontier scout who was handy with a gun and is credited with many feats of daring and with saving several lives during the Indian conflicts of the West. This tobacco chewing, hard drinking woman in men's clothes is also remembered as a saint by the citizens of Deadwood, South Dakota, where she nursed those suffering during an outbreak of smallpox.

BROCCOLI CHEDDAR BAKE

1 (10¾ ounce) can Cheddar cheese soup

½ cup milk

4 cups cooked broccoli, chopped

1 (2.8 ounce) can French's® fried onions

In 1½ quart casserole dish mix soup, milk, broccoli and ½ can onions. Bake for 25 minutes at 250 degrees. Stir. Sprinkle remaining onions over broccoli mixture. Bake five minutes more. Makes 6 servings.

BROCCOLI SUPREME

1 (10 ounce) package frozen broccoli

½ cup low-fat chicken broth

3 tablespoons low-fat salad dressing

2 teaspoons instant minced onion

Place broccoli in saucepan. Stir remaining ingredients together. Add to broccoli. Simmer covered, stirring occasionally until broccoli is defrosted. Uncover and continue to simmer, stirring occasionally until most of liquid has evaporated. Makes 3 servings.

NOT JUST ONIONS

12 to 15 small white onions

5 tablespoons butter

2 tablespoons sugar

Peel onions, add water to cover and cook until tender. Drain. Melt butter and sugar in skillet, add onions and cook over low heat 15 minutes, stirring occasionally. Makes 6 servings.

For nearly 25 years **LUCILLE BALL** *was one of the most influential women in television. She raised slapstick comedy to a high art and became known all over the world by just one name, Lucy. She and husband Desi Arnaz spent $5,000 of their own money to produce the pilot for "I Love Lucy" to convince CBS to take it. It is still delighting television audiences in reruns.*

FRENCH FRIED ONIONS

½ cup milk

4 large mild onions

½ cup flour

½ teaspoon salt

Peel onions, cut in ¼ inch slices, and separate into rings. Dip in milk and dip in flour with salt. Fry 4 to 6 minutes in deep oil heated to 370 degrees. Drain on paper towels and sprinkle with salt.

PEAS WITH CELERY AND ONION

1 cup celery, sliced diagonally

2 (10 ounce) packages frozen peas

⅓ cup thinly sliced onion

¼ cup butter

Add celery to ½ cup boiling water and cook 3 minutes. Add peas and onions, return to boil rapidly for 5 minutes, or until peas are tender. Drain and add butter. Makes 6 servings.

FRIED PEPPERS AND ONIONS

2 green bell peppers, sliced

1 large onion, sliced

3 tablespoons margarine

1 teaspoon salt

Combine all ingredients in nonstick skillet. Simmer covered over medium heat for 2 minutes. Uncover and cook until crisp and tender. Makes 4 servings.

JEANNE KIRKPATRICK was born in Oklahoma and educated at Columbia University and Paris University. She became professor of government in 1978 at Georgetown University, where she was noted for her hawkish anti-Communist defense stance and advocate of a new Latin American and Pacific oriented diplomatic strategy. She was appointed permanent representative to the United Nations by President Reagan in 1981 and remained there until 1985. She had been a Democrat, but joined the Republican Party in 1985.

MARY FALLIN *was elected in 1994 as not only Oklahoma's first woman Lieutenant Governor, but as the first Republican in that post. In 1998 she was re-elected by a margin of almost three to one. When she was in the Oklahoma State Legislature she received the American Legislative Exchange Council's Legislator of the Year Award. She served as Chairman of the National Conference of Lieutenant Governors during her first term. She has been extremely active as Lieutenant Governor.*

CRISPY FRIED BANANA PEPPERS

6 banana peppers

1½ cups cold water

1 cup cold milk

1 cup flour

Split peppers, remove seeds. Let sit in cold water 10 minutes. Remove from water, put in cold milk. Let sit 10 more minutes. Then roll in flour. Return to milk and then roll in flour. Deep fat fry in 360 degree oil. Drain on paper towels. Makes 6 servings.

GOLDEN PARMESAN POTATOES

½ stick butter

½ cup flour

½ cup Parmesan cheese

6 medium potatoes, quartered

Melt butter in baking dish. Mix flour and cheese in paper bag. Add moistened potatoes and shake. Place in baking dish and bake at 350 degrees for 50 to 60 minutes. Salt and pepper (optional). Makes 4 to 6 servings.

CHEESY SHOESTRINGS

1 (5 ounce) can shoestring potatoes

¼ cup Cheddar cheese

½ cup Parmesan cheese

Empty shoestring potatoes into shallow baking dish. Sprinkle with cheese. Bake at 350 degrees until toasty.

BAKED POTATO SLICES

4 medium potatoes

3 tablespoons margarine, melted

½ cup finely crushed corn flakes

1 teaspoon salt

Peel and slice potatoes ¼ inch thick. Place on cookie sheet, pour margarine over potatoes. Mix corn flakes and salt. Sprinkle over potatoes. Bake at 375 degrees until tender. Makes 4 to 6 servings.

DON'T PEEL COTTAGE FRIES

6 large Idaho potatoes

1 tablespoon salt

1 teaspoon pepper

Oil

Wash potatoes and pat dry. Cut lengthwise. Slice ¼ inch thick. Drop potatoes into deep-fat fryer at 360 degrees. Cook until golden brown. Drain and add salt and pepper. Makes 6 servings.

OVEN FRIED POTATOES

3 baking potatoes

1 tablespoon butter, melted

¼ teaspoon salt

⅛ teaspoon pepper

Peel potatoes and cut into thin slices. Place sliced potatoes on a greased baking sheet. Sprinkle with butter and salt and pepper. Bake at 350 degrees for 30 minutes. Makes 4 to 6 servings.

MAYA ANGELOU, author and poet, was San Francisco's first black streetcar conductor. At the request of Martin Luther King, Jr., she served as northern coordinator for the Southern Leadership Council in 1960–61. Her first volume of autobiography, I Know Why the Caged Bird Sings, *in 1971, was a best seller and was nominated for the National Book Award. In 1977 she was nominated for an Emmy for her role in* Roots. *She read the inaugural poem, "On the Pulse of Morning," on President Bill Clinton's Inauguration Day.*

MEXICAN HASH BROWNS

1 (5.5 ounce) package hash brown
   potatoes with onions
1 (4 ounce) can chopped green chiles,
   drained
1 cup shredded Monterey Jack cheese
3 tablespoons margarine

Cover potatoes with boiling water. Let stand 5 minutes. Drain thoroughly. Layer half each of the potatoes, chiles, and cheese into ungreased 8 x 8 x 2 inch baking dish. Dot with half of the margarine. Repeat with remaining ingredients. Cover and bake 20 minutes at 350 degrees. Uncover and bake until golden brown. Makes 4 servings.

REDUCED FAT POTATO SKINS

4 potatoes, baked
2 tablespoons light butter or margarine
8 ounces grated reduced fat Cheddar
   cheese
1 cup fat-free sour cream

Cut each potato into quarters lengthwise. Scoop out pulp ¼ inch from potato skin. Spread butter inside potato. Place on cookie sheet. Bake at 425 degrees for 10 minutes. Remove from oven and place cheese and sour cream on each quarter. Return to oven and bake until cheese melts. Makes 4 to 6 servings.

In 1996 **SHANNON LUCID** *from Bethany, Oklahoma, spent 188 days in space, a record for women and for United States astronauts. She has spent a total of 223 days (5,354 hours) in space, most time for a non-Russian and most for a woman. She was the first woman to receive the Congressional Space Medal of Honor.*

DELICIOUS CREAMED POTATOES

¼ pound butter

3 cups half and half

10 cold boiled potatoes, sliced thin

Put butter in large skillet. Add half and half and heat on low heat. Drop the sliced potatoes into the mixture. Sprinkle with salt and pepper. Simmer until milk is absorbed. Turn very carefully only once. This takes about an hour. Serve hot. Makes 8 servings.

PERFECT MASHED POTATOES

2 pounds red potatoes

½ cup whipping cream

½ cup butter

1 teaspoon salt

Peel and quarter potatoes. Place in saucepan. Cover potatoes with water. Bring to a boil. Lower heat and cook until potatoes are soft. Drain. Mash potatoes gradually adding cream, butter, and salt. Makes 6 servings.

ISADORA DUNCAN rejected the stylized, artificial movements of traditional ballet, improvised her own movements, danced to music (not written for dance) of the great composers, and wore costumes patterned on classical paintings and statues. Her free-flowing costumes and naturalistic movements heralded the new art form known as modern dance. In 1927 she was strangled to death as one of her long scarves was caught in the wheel of her open automobile in Nice, France.

SKINNY MASHED POTATOES

5 large potatoes, peeled and cubed

3½ cups chicken broth

½ teaspoon pepper

In saucepan, place potatoes and broth. Heat to a boil. Cover and cook over medium heat until potatoes are tender. Drain potatoes, reserving broth. Mash potatoes with 1¼ cups broth and pepper, if needed. Add additional broth until potatoes are desired consistency. Makes 6 servings.

VEGETABLE COMBO STIR-FRY

2 tablespoons butter or margarine

4 small new potatoes, quartered

1 pound fresh snow peas

1 onion, sliced and separated into rings

Melt butter in skillet and add potatoes. Stir-fry on medium heat 10 minutes or until potatoes are golden and crisp-tender. Add snow peas, onion and salt. Stir-fry 5 to 7 minutes or until peas are crisp-tender. Serve immediately. Makes 6 servings.

In 1983 **WILMA MANKILLER** *was elected deputy principal chief of the Cherokee Nation. When the principal chief became head of the Bureau of Indian Affairs in 1985, she became the first woman to serve as chief of a major Native American tribe. In 1987 she was elected in her own right and reelected in 1991. She was inducted into the National Women's Hall of Fame in 1993.*

SPEEDY SWEET POTATOES

1 (17 ounce) can sweet potatoes

¼ cup honey

2 tablespoons brown sugar

2 tablespoons butter

Drain sweet potatoes; arrange in greased shallow baking dish. In small saucepan, combine honey, brown sugar, and butter. Bring to a boil, stirring. Pour over sweet potatoes. Bake at 375 degrees for 30 minutes. Makes 4 servings.

BAKED ACORN SQUASH

1 medium acorn squash

2 tablespoons butter, melted

¼ teaspoon salt

½ tablespoon corn syrup

Scrub squash. Cut in half lengthwise. Scrape out seeds and stringy portion with spoon. Brush each half with butter. Sprinkle each half with ⅛ teaspoon of salt. Arrange cut sides down in a baking pan. Bake at 350 degrees for 30 minutes, then turn, cut sides up and brush with butter and corn syrup. Bake for 30 minutes more. Makes 2 servings.

RUTH STAPLETON, an evangelist and faith healer, is the younger sister of former President Jimmy Carter, and was influential in his conversion to Christianity. Unlike many of her fellow Southern Baptists, she cooperated with other Christians, including Roman Catholics. In the 1976 presidential campaign she addressed the National Press Club in Washington, DC, on her brother's behalf—the first time it had listened to a woman preacher.

SACAJAWEA *traveled thousands of miles of wilderness with the Lewis and Clark Expedition to the Pacific Northwest from 1804–1806, many of them with her carrying her infant son on her back. She had been allowed to accompany her husband who had been hired as an interpreter. Her presence and kinship with the Indians helped gain cooperation of some of the Native Americans they encountered. Her courage and fortitude are commemorated in the new gold colored one dollar U.S. coin.*

STOVE TOP SQUASH

3 yellow squash

2 tablespoons olive oil

1 medium onion, chopped

Grate yellow squash. Heat olive oil in a non-stick skillet. Add squash and onion. Cook over medium heat. Lower heat; cook 15 to 30 minutes, stirring occasionally. Makes 4 servings.

BROWN SUGAR BAKED SQUASH

1 squash, cut in half

2 tablespoons butter

2 tablespoons brown sugar

¼ teaspoon salt

Wash squash and remove seeds. Place in shallow pan and ¼ inch water. Bake at 350 degrees for 20 minutes. Mix butter, sugar, and salt. Spread over inside of squash. Bake 20 minutes more. Makes 2 servings.

BAKED MASHED SQUASH

1 medium acorn squash, halved and seeded

1 tablespoon maple syrup

½ teaspoon pumpkin pie spice

½ teaspoon butter-flavored salt

Place squash halves cut sides down on baking sheet. Bake at 400 degrees for 30 minutes. Scoop out squash into mixing bowl. Beat with electric mixer. Stir in syrup, pumpkin pie spice, and salt. Makes 4 servings.

SPINACH DELIGHT

1 (10 ounce) package frozen spinach

2 cups salad dressing

½ cup chopped green onions

1 cup finely chopped parsley

Cook spinach in salted water until tender. Drain and mash. Mix with other ingredients and let set for 24 hours. Keep refrigerated. Makes 3 cups.

BUTTERY TASTE SPINACH

1 (10 ounce) package frozen spinach, defrosted

¼ cup water

½ teaspoon butter-flavored salt

Combine all ingredients in saucepan. Cook covered for 3 minutes. Makes 2 servings.

FRIED GREEN TOMATOES

4 large green tomatoes

½ cup flour

1 teaspoon salt

Bacon drippings

Cut tomatoes into ¼ inch slices. Combine flour and salt. Dredge tomato slices in flour mixture. Place in skillet containing hot bacon drippings. Fry slowly until brown. Makes 6 servings.

POCAHONTAS, daughter of an Indian chief, is supposed to have saved the life of Captain John Smith, founder of the English colony at Jamestown, Virginia, in 1607. As he was to be beheaded she threw her body over his and convinced her father to spare him. She later was kidnapped by the English and held hostage for peace. She married John Rolfe, one of the settlers, and on a visit to England, she contracted smallpox and died at the age of 21.

BAKED STUFFED TOMATOES

6 tomatoes

2 tablespoons chopped green pepper

½ cup finely chopped celery

1 tablespoon finely chopped onion

Remove tops and scoop out tomatoes. Combine tomato pulp with remaining ingredients in saucepan and cook until thick. Stuff tomatoes. Place in muffin tins so tomatoes will stay erect and bake at 375 degrees 25 to 30 minutes. Makes 6 servings.

SEASONED BAKED TOMATOES

3 large tomatoes, cut crosswise into halves

3 tablespoons seasoned bread crumbs

2 teaspoons olive oil

1 teaspoon onion powder

Place tomatoes cut-sides up on baking sheet. Combine remaining ingredients and use to stuff tomatoes. Bake at 375 degrees for 12 minutes. Makes 6 servings.

COOKED GREENS

1 pound ham hock

2 cups water

1 teaspoon salt

3 pounds collard greens

Simmer meat in water for 45 minutes. Add salt and collard greens. Cover and cook for 30 minutes or until tender. Makes 4 servings.

ANNIE OAKLEY, "Little Sure Shot," (1860-1926) was one of the world's greatest markswomen and a flamboyant entertainer. She could shoot a dime tossed into the air and hit the edge of a playing card at 30 paces. During a legendary performance in Berlin, she shot a cigarette out of the mouth of Crown Prince William. For years, a reminder of Annie's exploits was the use of the term "Annie Oakley" to denote a complimentary pass. The holes punched in the ticket recalled the bullet holes she fired into playing cards during her performances.

QUICK AND EASY BROILED ZUCCHINI

3 zucchini, cut in half lengthwise

1½ tablespoons butter or margarine, melted

Salt and pepper

3 tablespoons grated Parmesan cheese

Place zucchini cut side up in lightly greased broiler pan. Brush with butter and sprinkle with salt, pepper and cheese. Broil 6 to 8 inches from heat for 12 minutes or until tender. Makes 3 servings.

HOLLANDAISE SAUCE

4 egg yolks

2 tablespoons lemon juice

½ pound butter, melted

Salt and pepper

In top half of double boiler, beat egg yolks and stir in lemon juice. Cook very slowly. Add butter, a little at a time, stirring constantly with a wooden spoon. Add salt and pepper. Continue cooking until thickened. Makes 1 cup.

MOCK HOLLANDAISE SAUCE

1 (10¾ ounce) can cream of chicken soup

¼ cup mayonnaise

1 teaspoon lemon juice

In saucepan, add soup, mayonnaise, and lemon juice. Cook over low heat, stirring occasionally, until heated through. Serve over vegetables.

She had drawn pictures as a child, but **GRANDMA MOSES** *did not start painting until 1938 when she was in her late 70's. Her first pictures sold in a drugstore in Hoosick Falls, New York, but she went on to international fame with her paintings of what she called "old timey" farm life in New York and Virginia. She had 15 one-woman shows in the U. S. and Europe before her death at age 101 in 1961.*

Senior class president and prom queen **ROSIE O'DONNELL** *dreamed of being an actress, not a comedienne. However, with her comedy she won the Star Search competition five times. After several successful movies, she switched to TV to be a full time mother to her adopted son. Newsweek called her the "Queen of Nice," a talk show host who is irreverent, frank, gracious, and hilarious without being trashy. She is an everywoman for millions of daytime TV diehards looking for someone they can relate to. She champions many causes especially prevention of breast cancer.*

CREAM SAUCE

2 tablespoons butter

2 tablespoons flour

½ teaspoon salt

1 cup milk

In small saucepan, melt butter over low heat. Blend in flour and salt. Stir constantly until smooth and bubbly. Remove from heat. Add milk gradually and return to heat, stirring all the while. Bring to a boil for 1 minute. Makes 1 cup.

VEGGIE BATTER

2 eggs

1 cup beer

1¼ cups flour

In bowl add eggs, beer, and flour. Beat until smooth. Dip any fresh vegetables in batter and deep fat fry. Makes 2½ cups.

HERB-BUTTERED SPAGHETTI

1 (4 ounce) package spaghetti, cooked

2 tablespoons margarine or butter

½ teaspoon dried basil

2 tablespoons grated Parmesan cheese

Combine cooked spaghetti, butter, dried basil and Parmesan cheese. Heat until hot.

CHILI SPAGHETTI

1 (4 ounce) package spaghetti

1 (15 ounce) can no bean chili

1 cup grated Cheddar cheese

Cook spaghetti and drain. Keep warm. In sauce-pan add chili and heat over medium heat. Pour over spaghetti. Sprinkle cheese over top. Makes 4 servings.

CHICKEN PASTA PRIMAVERA

2 cups chopped fresh vegetables

2 cups cooked linguine, drained

1 (6 ounce) package grilled chicken breast strips

½ cup grated Parmesan cheese

Cook and stir vegetables in a little olive oil in large skillet for 5 minutes. Add linguine and chicken breast strips. Cook for 3 minutes. Stir in cheese. Makes 3 servings.

QUICK PASTA SKILLET

1 pound ground beef, cooked

3 cups cooked mostaccioli

1 (28 ounce) jar spaghetti sauce

1 (8 ounce) package shredded mozzarella cheese

In large skillet brown ground beef, cooked mostaccioli, spaghetti sauce, and cheese. Cook on low heat and simmer 15 minutes. Sprinkle with Parmesan cheese (optional).

*In the late 1870 **ESTHER McQUIGG MORRIS** was elected justice of the peace in South Pass City, Wyoming, the first woman in the world to hold that office. At age 55 in 1869, this charming, reserved lady held a tea party for the candidates for the state legislature. She got a promise from each of the candidates that if elected, he would introduce a bill for women's voting rights. The winner kept his word, and surprisingly, on December 10, 1869, for the first time anywhere on earth, women were given the legal right to vote.*

ANN LANDERS (born Esther Pauline Friedman) and her identical twin sister, ABIGAIL VAN BUREN (Pauline Esther Friedman) have been writing syndicated newspaper advice columns longer and have reached more readers than any other such columnists. Ann Landers began her column for the Chicago Sun-Times Syndicate in 1955 in 26 newspapers. She receives over 1,000 letters per week seeking her sometimes biting, sometimes humorous advice. Dear Abby began in 1956 for the McNaught Syndicate on the West Coast.

FETTUCINE ALL' ALFREDO

1 (8 ounce) package fettucine, cooked

4 tablespoons butter

2 cups whipping cream

1 cup grated Parmesan cheese

Put cooked fettucine, butter and cream in saucepan, heat thoroughly. Add cheese and toss gently. Makes 4 servings.

FETTUCINE ALFREDO

1 (4 ounce) package fettucine, cooked

3 tablespoons whipping cream

1/3 cup grated Parmesan cheese

1 tablespoon butter

Place cooked fettuccine in saucepan. Add cream, Parmesan cheese and butter. Toss gently. Heat on low heat until hot. Makes 4 servings.

TOO BUSY FETTUCINE ALFREDO

1 (16 ounce) package fettucine

1/2 cup butter

2 cups grated Parmesan cheese

1/2 teaspoon pepper

Cook and drain fettucine. Add butter, Parmesan cheese and pepper. Toss thoroughly until cheese melts. Makes 6 servings.

VEGETABLE ALFREDO

1 (8 ounce) package bow tie pasta, uncooked

1 (16 ounce) bag frozen mix vegetables

1 (6 ounce) package alfredo pasta sauce mix

½ teaspoon pepper

In a large saucepan, cook pasta according to package directions. Add vegetables during last 5 minutes of pasta cooking. Drain and return to saucepan. Meanwhile, in medium saucepan, prepare sauce according to package directions. Stir sauce into vegetables and pasta. Cook until heated through. Sprinkle with pepper before serving. Makes 4 servings.

TORTELLINI WITH CREAM SAUCE

1 (9 ounce) package meat-filled tortellini

1 cup whipping cream

4 teaspoons sun-dried tomato paste

¼ cup chopped parsley

Cook tortellini according to package directions. Drain and set aside. In the same saucepan, bring cream to a boil over medium heat. Cook for 5 minutes, stirring frequently. Remove from heat, add tomato paste and whisk until well blended. Add tortellini to mixture. Toss to coat. Sprinkle with parsley before serving. Makes 4 servings.

*When **BETTY FORD**, wife of the 38th President of the United States, Gerald Ford, was diagnosed with breast cancer, she became a vocal advocate for increased awareness about this and other women's health issues. After her recovery from chemical dependency, she helped found the Betty Ford Center in California to assist people in recovering from alcohol and drug addiction. It is regarded as the premier treatment facility in the nation.*

THREE CHEESE PASTA DISH

1 pound sausage

1 large onion

1 (28 ounce) jar three cheese pasta sauce

4½ cups cooked tube macaroni

In skillet over medium heat, cook sausage and onion until sausage is brown. Pour off fat. Add pasta sauce. Heat to a boil. Serve over macaroni. Makes 4 servings.

RAVIOLI TASTY TOSS

1 (9 ounce) package fresh spinach ravioli

4 tablespoons butter, melted

⅓ cup chopped parsley

½ cup grated Parmesan cheese

In a large saucepan of rapidly boiling, lightly salted water, cook ravioli until just tender, 6 to 7 minutes. Drain well. Toss hot ravioli with melted butter, parsley, and Parmesan cheese. Serve immediately. Makes 4 servings.

CHEESY TORTELLINI

½ pound Velveeta® cheese, cubed

¼ cup milk

½ teaspoon nutmeg

1 (7 ounce) package cheese-filled tortellini, cooked and drained

In a saucepan, add cheese, milk, and nutmeg. Heat over low heat until cheese melts. Pour over cooked tortellini. Mix well.

SHIRLEY TEMPLE *became America's darling with her curly hairdo and became the number one box office attraction in motion pictures in 1935 at the age of seven. Her singing, dancing and acting tugged the heartstrings of an America still in the effects of the Depression. Dolls in her likeness were extremely popular and are now collectors' items. Later, as Shirley Temple Black, she became a delegate to the United Nations and U.S. Ambassador to Ghana.*

POTLUCK SUPPER

1 (14 ounce) package deluxe macaroni
   and cheese dinner

2 cups chopped cooked chicken

1/2 cup sour cream

Prepare macaroni and cheese dinner as directed
on package. Add cooked chicken and sour
cream. Mix well. Heat thoroughly, stirring occasionally. Makes 5 servings.

ONE DISH MEAL

1 pound ground beef

1 (15 ounce) can corn, drained

3 cups macaroni and cheese

Brown ground beef, drain. Put in baking dish
and pour drained corn and macaroni and cheese
on top. Bake at 350 degrees for 40 minutes. It's
great.

MAC 'N CHEESE FIX UP

1 (14 ounce) package deluxe macaroni
   and cheese dinner

1/2 pound ground beef, cooked and
   drained

1/3 cup taco sauce

Prepare macaroni and cheese according to directions on package. Combine all ingredients in
saucepan. Heat through. Makes 4 servings.

MARIE SKLODOWSKA CURIE, the discoverer of radium with her husband, Pierre, received two Nobel Prizes. They did not patent their discovery which would have assured them a personal fortune, but shared their information with the American medical community so it could be used to treat disease. She died of leukemia brought on by radiation exposure.

TWISTY MACARONI AND CHEESE

1 (12 ounce) package corkscrew
    macaroni, cooked

1 cup broccoli cuts, cooked

1 (8 ounce) jar pasteurized cheese spread

2 sliced bacon, cooked and crumbled

In a saucepan, combine macaroni, broccoli and cheese. Cook and stir over medium heat until heated through. Sprinkle bacon over mixture before serving.

CRUSTLESS QUICHE

1 (10 ounce) package frozen chopped
    spinach

4 eggs, beaten

¾ cup feta cheese, crumbled

½ cup milk

Cook and drain spinach. Add beaten eggs, cheese, and milk. Mix well. Pour in baking dish. Bake at 325 degrees for 35 minutes, or until set. Makes 6 servings.

SWISS CHEESE PIE

1²/₃ cups milk

4 eggs

½ cup finely chopped smoked sliced beef

1 cup shredded Swiss cheese

In mixing bowl, beat milk, eggs and salt, add beef and Swiss cheese. Mix well. Pour into 9 inch unbaked pie shell. Bake at 350 degrees for 30 to 40 minutes. Allow pie to stand 10 minutes before serving. Makes 4 to 6 servings.

MARTINA NAVRATILOVA *defected from Czechoslovakia to America in 1975. As a tennis player she became one of the best-paid and most famous female athletes in the world. She won more singles (167) and more doubles (163) tournaments than any other woman. In 1984 she had a winning streak of 74 matches. She was one of the first world-class athletes to not hide the fact that she was homosexual.*

PIONEER HOMEMADE NOODLES

1 cup sifted flour

1 teaspoon salt

2 eggs, beaten

1 tablespoon milk

Sift flour and salt together. Add eggs and stir. Add enough flour to make a thick mixture. Add milk and work into the rest of the mixture. Dump out onto floured board and knead until enough flour is worked in to make soft dough and you are able to roll it out without sticking. After rolling, dust with flour and let set 30 minutes, roll dough jelly roll fashion. Cut into thin strips, shake out and let dry. Cook in hot chicken or beef broth. Makes 6 servings.

NEVER FAIL DUMPLINGS

2 cups flour

2 teaspoons (heaping) baking powder

½ teaspoon salt

1 cup milk

Combine all ingredients and mix well. Drop from tablespoon into boiling chicken broth. Boil for 15 minutes. Put cover on tight and boil for 5 minutes longer.

MARGARET BOURKE-WHITE contributed greatly to the rise of photojournalism as an art form. She was one of the first photographers to enter the death camps at the end of World War II. On assignment for Life *she shot one of her most famous photographs, "Gandhi at His Spinning Wheel."*

CHEESE BAKED RICE

2½ cups cooked rice

1 (7 ounce) can diced green chiles

2 cups sour cream

1 cup Cheddar cheese

Combine all ingredients in large bowl. Pour into a well-buttered baking dish. Bake at 350 degrees for 35 minutes. Makes 4 servings.

QUICK RICE PILAF

1 cup brown rice, uncooked

1 (10¾ ounce) can French onion soup, undiluted

1 (15 ounce) can beef consommé, undiluted

1 cup butter

Add rice, onion soup, beef consommé, and butter in casserole dish. Cover tight with aluminum foil. Bake at 350 degrees for 60 minutes. Makes 4 servings.

CHILI CHEESE PIE

2 (15½ ounce) cans chili

½ cup grated Cheddar cheese

¾ cup water

1 (6 ounce) package cornbread mix

Pour chili into an 8 inch square baking dish. Sprinkle with Cheddar cheese. Stir water into cornbread mix and beat until smooth. Pour cornbread batter over chili. Bake at 375 degrees for 30 minutes. Makes 6 servings.

GRACE KELLY was from a wealthy Philadelphia family. She was a leading lady of stately beauty and reserve in eleven motion pictures, and won an Academy Award in 1954 for The Country Girl. *On April 16, 1956, she married Ranier III, the ruling prince of Monaco and became Princess Grace of Monaco.*

DOUBLE-QUICK CHILI BAKE

1 (15½ ounce) can chili without beans

1 (12 ounce) can sweet peppers, drained

3 tablespoons chopped onion

3 tablespoons grated Cheddar cheese

Put chili into 9 inch baking dish. Top with pepper, onions, and cheese. Bake at 350 degrees for 20 minutes. Makes 4 servings.

QUICK-FIX TAMALES

8 frozen tamales

2 cups cooked chicken, diced

4 green onions, diced

12 ounces Longhorn cheese, shredded

Prepare tamales as directed on package. Place tamales in baking dish. Cover with chicken, onions, and cheese. Bake at 350 degrees for 5 minutes or until cheese melts. Makes 4 servings.

CHILI TAMALE CASSEROLE

1 (15 ounce) can tamales

1 (15 ounce) can chili con carne

½ cup grated cheese

½ cup chopped onion

Mash tamales with a fork. Mix well with chili con carne. Place in casserole and sprinkle with grated cheese and chopped onion. Microwave on high, covered loosely for 6 minutes. Makes 4 servings.

The first book of **ELIZABETH KUBLER ROSS,** On Death and Dying, *explored the process by which people cope with death—a subject long ignored. This psychiatrist has helped countless dying patients achieve a liberation of spirit and make the medical community more responsive to the emotional needs of the dying and their families.*

2-MINUTE ENCHILADAS

10 flour tortillas

1 cup grated Cheddar cheese

1 medium onion, chopped

1 (15 ounce) can enchilada sauce

Sprinkle each tortilla with cheese and onion. Roll tortillas and place seam side down in microwave safe dish. Pour enchilada sauce over tortillas. Cover and cook on high 2 minutes, or until cheese melts. Top with extra cheese before serving.

NO-FAT CHILE PIE

1 (4½ ounce) can green chiles, diced

2 cups grated non-fat pizza cheese

2 green onions, chopped

1 (4 ounce) container Egg Beaters®

Place green chiles in a 13 x 9 inch baking dish. Sprinkle with cheese and onions. Pour eggs over top. Bake at 350 degrees for 10 to 15 minutes. Makes 6 servings.

HOT DOGGIE ROLL-UPS

1 (8 count) can refrigerated crescent dinner rolls

American cheese cut into strips

8 hot dogs

Separate crescent rolls into 8 triangles. Top with a strip of cheese and a hot dog and roll up. Place on greased cookie sheet. Bake at 375 degrees for 10 to 12 minutes. Makes 8.

AVA GARDNER was the daughter of a poor Southern sharecropper, but she went on to achieve fame as one of the most beautiful women in motion pictures, known for her husky voice and seductiveness. In 1953 she was nominated for an Oscar for her performance opposite Clark Gable in Mogambo. She married Mickey Rooney and Artie Shaw, but was best known for her stormy marriage and relationship with Frank Sinatra.

HAMBURGER ROLLS

1 pound ground beef

1½ cups grated Cheddar cheese

1 (2.8 ounce) can onions

2 (8 count) cans refrigerated crescent
   rolls

Brown ground beef and drain. Mix cheese and
onions and crumble into beef. Put 1 tablespoon
of mixture onto each crescent roll. Fold over
the mixture. Place on ungreased cookie sheet.
Bake at 350 degrees for 8 minutes or until light
brown. Makes 16 servings.

QUICK STUFFED PEPPERS

3 green peppers

1 pound ground beef, browned and
   drained

1 (15 ounce) can Spanish rice

2 tablespoons ketchup

Cut green peppers in half and remove pulp.
Steam peppers in 1 inch of water for 5 minutes.
Cool. Add Spanish rice and ketchup to cooked
ground beef. Spoon mixture into green pepper.
Place in baking pan and bake at 350 degrees for
25 minutes.

*JENNY LIND
(1820-87),
the "Swedish
Nightingale," was
born of humble
parents in
Stockholm. She
entered the court
theatre school of
singing at age
nine. After
lessons in Paris,
the soprano
attained a great
international
popularity. She
devoted most of
her earnings to
founding and
endowing musical
scholarships and
charities in
Sweden and
England.*

EVERYONE'S FAVORITE CHICKEN CASSEROLE

2½ or 3 pounds chicken, cooked

2 (6 ounce) boxes stuffing mix

1½ (10¾ ounce) cans cream of chicken soup

1½ cups carton plain yogurt

Boil chicken until done. Pull apart from bone and set aside. Fix stuffing according to directions on box. Spread half of stuffing in the 2 quart baking dish. Cover stuffing with chicken. Spread soup and yogurt over chicken and sprinkle with the rest of the stuffing. Bake at 350 degrees for 45 minutes. Makes 6 servings.

TURKEY CHILI

1 pound ground turkey, cooked

2 (15 ounce) cans chili with beans

½ cup gratted cheese

¼ cup diced onion

In saucepan, put cooked turkey and chili. Cook over low heat until hot. Top with cheese and onion. Makes 4 servings.

JOSEPHINE BAKER was a black American singer and dancer who became a big star in Paris in the 1920's. She created a sensation at the Folies-Bergere by dancing seminude in a skirt made only of bananas. For her work during World War II with the Red Cross and the Resistance she was awarded the Croix de Guerre and the Legion of Honor with the rosette of the Resistance.

TURKEY TURNOVERS

1 (11.3 ounce) package refrigerated
    dinner rolls

2 tablespoons prepared honey mustard

3 ounces thinly sliced deli turkey breast

¾ cup broccoli coleslaw

Separate dinner rolls and place on lightly
floured surface. Roll each dinner roll into 3½
inch circle. Spread honey mustard lightly over
dinner rolls. Top with turkey and broccoli coleslaw. Fold dough over forming a half circle. Seal
edges. Put on sprayed cookie sheet. Bake at 425
degrees for 15 minutes. Makes 8 servings.

BAKED BEANS AND
PORK CHOPS

3 cups baked beans

2 cups tomatoes, chopped

½ cup packed brown sugar

6 pork chops

Combine beans, tomatoes, and brown sugar.
Mix well. Pour into baking dish, laying pork
chops on top. Bake at 350 degrees for 1 hour.
Makes 6 servings.

*A child of
former slaves,*
**MADAME C.
J. WALKER**
*became America's
first black self-
made female
millionaire by
creating and
marketing a line
of beauty and
hair products to
African-American
women. By 1919
her company was
the largest and
most lucrative of
its kind in the
United States.*

SAUCY BAKED BEANS

20 pepperoni slices, quartered

1 small onion, chopped

2 (16 ounce) cans pork and beans

½ cup barbecue sauce

In a saucepan, cook pepperoni and onion until onion is tender. Stir in remaining ingredients and bring to a boil. Reduce heat, simmer uncovered for 10-15 minutes, stirring occasionally. Makes 6 to 8 servings.

HEAVEN-IN-A-SKILLET

6 slices bacon

3 cups frozen hash brown potatoes with onions and peppers

1 cup shredded Monterey Jack cheese

4 eggs

Cook bacon until crisp. Drain and reserve 2 tablespoons of drippings in skillet. Set bacon aside. Cook frozen hash brown potatoes in reserved drippings until golden. Crumble 2 slices of bacon and stir into potatoes. Sprinkle cheese over potatoes. Place remaining 4 slices of bacon in an X on top of cheese. Carefully break one egg into each triangle formed by bacon. Cover and cook over medium heat 6 minutes or until eggs are set. Makes 4 servings.

The pioneering role in investigative journalism of **IDA M. TARBELL** *spurred government investigations of Standard Oil and led to the breakup of their monopoly in 1911 under the Sherman Anti-Trust Act. Ironically her father had made a fortune supplying wooden tanks for the early petroleum industry.*

QUICK BEEF GOULASH

1 pound ground beef

1 onion, chopped

2 cups chopped tomatoes

8 ounces macaroni, cooked

Cook ground beef and onion in skillet until meat is done. Drain. Add tomatoes and macaroni, salt and pepper. Cook on low heat for 15 minutes.

BAKED CHILE CORN CASSEROLE

1 (15.25 ounce) can whole kernel corn, drained

1 (15.25 ounce) can creamed corn

1 (8 ounce) package cream cheese

1 (4 ounce) can green chiles, undrained

Butter 1½ quart casserole dish. Combine both cans of corn and cream cheese in saucepan. Heat over low heat, stirring constantly until cheese melts. Add chiles and stir well. Pour into casserole dish. Bake at 300 degrees for 15 to 20 minutes. Optional: top with buttered bread crumbs before baking.

HELEN TAUSSIG (1898-1896), a pediatric cardiologist, is one of two doctors responsible for performing the first "blue baby" operation in 1944. She was the first physician to warn against the birth defects caused by use of the drug thalidomide in pregnant women. Dr. Taussig also received the United States of America Medal of Freedom for her contributions to cardiology. Her other honors include recognition by the French, Italian and Peruvian governments.

CHILI-FRANK BURRITOS

4 (7-inch) tortillas

4 slices of cheese

4 chili-stuffed frankfurters

Wrap tortillas in foil. Heat in a 375 degree oven for 5 minutes. On top of each tortilla arrange one slice of cheese and one frankfurter. Fold in ends of tortillas. Roll up and wrap in foil. Bake at 375 degrees for 15 minutes. Makes 4 servings.

SOUTH OF THE BORDER BUNDLES

1 (12 ounce) jar chunky salsa

2 cups cubed Velveeta®

3 cups chopped cooked chicken

4 (8-inch) flour tortillas

In a medium saucepan, combine salsa and cheese. Cook over medium heat until cheese melts. Set aside 1¼ cups mixture. Stir chicken into remaining mixture. Spoon some of the chicken mixture down the center of each tortilla. Roll up tortillas. Place the filled tortillas, seam side down, in a greased 8 x 8 x 2 inch baking dish. Cover with foil. Bake at 375 degrees for 15 to 20 minutes. Reheat sauce and pour over enchiladas.

SYLVIA BEACH (1887-1962) an American-born publisher and bookseller, was a fixture in the Paris intellectual community during the 1920's and 1930's. She is famous for publishing (1922) James Joyce's work Ulysses *in book form, after established publishers, who considered portions of it obscene, had rejected it. Her bookshop, Shakespeare & Co., was a literary mecca for expatriate American and British writers, including F. Scott Fitzgerald and Ernest Hemmingway. Her shop closed in 1941 because of the German occupation of Paris.*

Sweet
Aromas

breads

biscuits

rolls

Famous
First Women

34. ELIZABETH CADY STANTON was the first woman to be a witness at a Congressional hearing when she addressed the District Commission of the U.S. Senate in 1869. She was trying to keep women in the District of Columbia from being debarred from voting.

35. HATTIE OPHELIA CARAWAY, a Jonesboro, Arkansas, Democrat, was appointed to fill the vacancy in the U.S. Senate caused by the death of her husband. In 1932 she became the first woman elected to the Senate and was re-elected in 1938.

36. LEE ANN BREEDLOVE was the first woman to drive over 300 miles an hour. She drove the jet powered Spirit of America at Bonneville Salt Flats in Utah for two runs over the one mile course at an average of 308.56 miles per hour.

37. DIANE CRUMP of Oldsman, Florida, was the first woman to ride in a para mutuel race on a flat track at Hialeah, Florida, in 1969. In 1970 she was the first woman to ride in the Kentucky Derby, finishing 15th in a 17 horse field on Fathom.

38. On April 6, 1978, President Jimmy Carter nominated MARGARET ANN BREWER to become the first woman general in the U.S. Marine Corps. Brigadier General Brewer was sworn in on May 1, 1978, as director of the Division of Information.

39. SARAH WALDRAKE and RACHEL SUMMERS became the first women federal government employees when they went to work at the Mint in Philadelphia in 1795. They were paid 50 cents a day as adjusters to weigh gold coins.

40. MABEL GILMORE REINECKE was the first woman internal revenue collector. She was appointed by President Warren G. Harding and served as collector of Internal Revenue from the First District of Illinois from June 1, 1923 to March 31, 1929.

CINNAMON COFFEE CAKE

2 (10 count) cans refrigerated biscuits

½ cup butter, melted

⅓ cup packed brown sugar

1 teaspoon cinnamon

Overlap biscuits in 9-inch cake pan in a spiral fashion. Combine butter, sugar and cinnamon. Spread over biscuits. Bake at 350 degrees for 30 minutes. Sprinkle with chopped nuts (optional).

QUICK DOUGHNUTS

1 (10 count) can refrigerated biscuits

Oil

3 tablespoons sugar

1½ teaspoons cinnamon

Make doughnuts by cutting out centers of each biscuit. Heat oil in deep fat fryer or skillet. Gently drop doughnut in hot oil; cook until lightly brown. Turn and brown second side. Remove; drain, roll in cinnamon and sugar mixture. Makes 5 servings

---

SOPAIPILLAS

4 cups sifted flour

1 tablespoon baking powder

1 teaspoon salt

3 tablespoons shortening

In a bowl, combine flour, baking powder, and salt. Blend in shortening. Add enough water to make a soft dough. Roll out dough to pie crust thickness. Cut into 3 inch squares. Deep fry in hot oil until golden brown.

SANDRA DAY O'CONNOR was admitted to the bar in California, but took up practice in Arizona where she became Assistant Attorney General (1965–69) and then state senator. She was superior court judge of Maricopa County and judge of the Arizona Court of Appeals. In 1981 President Ronald Reagan nominated her an associate justice on the United States Supreme Court, the first woman to attain that office. She has taken a full share in the work of the court and has shown an independent spirit.

QUICK CINNAMON BREAD

2 (10 count) cans refrigerated biscuits

1/3 cup butter

1 1/2 teaspoons cinnamon

3/4 cup packed brown sugar

Cut each uncooked biscuit into fourths and place in greased loaf pan. In saucepan put butter, cinnamon, and brown sugar. Heat to a boil. Pour over biscuits. Bake at 350 degrees for 25 to 30 minutes.

CHERRY FILLED CRESCENT ROLLS

1 (8 count) can crescent rolls

1 1/2 cups cherry pie filling

1/2 cup confectioner's sugar

Unroll crescent rolls. Place 2 tablespoons cherry pie filling in center of each roll. Roll up dough. Bake according to directions on can. Sprinkle with confectioner's sugar. Makes 4 servings.

EASY-DOES-IT COFFEE ROLLS

1 cup pecans, chopped

1 cup packed brown sugar

2 (10 count) cans refrigerated biscuits

1/2 cup butter

Combine pecans and brown sugar. Dip each biscuit in melted butter and then roll in brown sugar mixture. Place on cookie sheet. Bake at 350 degrees for 20 minutes.

DIANA VREELAND *was for many years the most influential fashion editor in the United States. She began with a column in* Harper's Bazaar *in 1936 and became its fashion editor the next year. During the 1960's, as editor of* Vogue *she was the presiding arbiter of women's fashions.*

CARAMEL-NUT BREAD

⅓ cup caramel topping

2 tablespoons margarine or butter, melted

½ cup chopped pecans or walnuts

1 (8 count) package refrigerated breadsticks

In a 9 x 1½ inch round baking pan stir together topping and melted butter. Sprinkle with nuts. Separate, but do not uncoil breadsticks. Arrange dough coils in pan on top of nuts. Bake uncovered at 350 degrees for 20 to 25 minutes. Let stand 3 minutes. Spread any remaining topping onto rolls. Serve warm.

HOT 'N' RISING ROLLS

18-24 frozen rolls

1 (4 serving) box cook and serve butterscotch pudding

1 stick margarine

½ cup packed brown sugar

Cut rolls in half while frozen. Place around bottom of bundt pan and place dry pudding over rolls. Heat margarine and brown sugar in a small sauce pan. Pour over dry pudding. Let rise. Bake at 325 degrees for 35 minutes. Cool 10-20 minutes before turning out on serving dish.

JEANA YEAGER was co-pilot of the Voyager when it made the first non-stop flight around the world without refueling in December, 1986. It took 9 days, 3 minutes, and 44 seconds for the 25,012 mile flight. When she and pilot Richard G. Rutan landed they had only five gallons of usable fuel left.

JUST-A-SNACK

6 flour tortillas, any size

¼ cup orange juice

Cinnamon

Sugar

Brush one side of each tortilla with orange juice. Sprinkle with cinnamon and sugar. Roll and microwave on high for 30 seconds. Makes 3 to 6 servings.

INDIAN FRY BREAD

3 cups flour

1¼ teaspoons baking powder

1⅓ cups warm water

¾ cup shortening

Mix flour and baking powder together. Mix with water. Knead until dough is soft. Shape and thin to a flat pancake 5 inches in diameter. Heat shortening in pan until hot. Put shaped pieces of dough in hot grease. Brown on both sides.

SESAME BREADSTICKS

1 (10 count) package refrigerated Parker House rolls

2 tablespoons margarine

1 tablespoon sesame seeds, toasted

Shape each roll into a pencil-like rope 10 inches long. Brush with margarine; sprinkle with sesame seeds. Place on baking sheet. Bake at 375 degrees for 9 to 10 minutes. Makes 10 breadsticks.

VIVIEN LEIGH, an English actress, was best known for her role as Scarlet O'Hara in the 1939 movie, Gone With The Wind, *a role she won over hundreds of other actresses in a nationwide search. She appeared in movies and on stage in both England and America. She was married to Laurence Olivier in 1937 when they performed together in "Hamlet."*

EVERYONE'S FAVORITE BACON STICKS

5 slices bacon, cut lengthwise in half
1/2 cup grated Parmesan cheese
10 thin breadsticks

Coat one side of bacon slice with cheese. Roll coated side of bacon diagonally around breadstick: roll breadstick in cheese. Repeat with remaining bacon, cheese, and breadsticks. Place bacon sticks on ungreased cookie sheet. Bake at 250 degrees for 1 hour or until golden brown. Makes 10 servings.

BISCUIT BITS WITH DEVILED HAM

1 (10 count) can refrigerated biscuits
1/4 cup butter or margarine
1 (4 1/2 ounce) can deviled ham
1/4 cup grated Parmesan cheese

Snip biscuits in quarters. Arrange in two 8 inch round baking dishes. Heat together butter and deviled ham, stirring until blended. Pour ham mixture over biscuit pieces. Sprinkle with Parmesan cheese. Bake at 400 degrees for 15 minutes, or until golden brown. Serve hot as snack or with a salad supper. Makes 40.

EMILY DAVISON, an English suffragette, was a militant member of the Women's Social and Political Union. Her activities included stone throwing and setting alight letterboxes. She resorted to hunger striking during her frequent imprisonments and was repeatedly force-fed. In the 1913 Derby, wearing a WSPU banner, she tried to catch the reins of the king's horse and was trampled underfoot. She died several days later of her injuries.

BACON BITS DROP BISCUITS

²/₃ cup milk

2 cups Bisquick®

¹/₃ cup crispy cooked diced bacon

Add milk all at once to Bisquick. Beat vigorously 20 strokes. Add bacon and mix well. Drop dough with spoon onto ungreased baking sheet. Bake at 450 degrees for 10 to 15 minutes. Makes 12 biscuits.

TIPPIE BISCUITS

4 cups Bisquick®

1 teaspoon oil

2 teaspoons sugar

1 (12 ounce) can beer at room temperature

Mix all the ingredients together and pour into greased muffin tins. Fill only ½ full. Let sit about 20 minutes. Bake at 400 degrees for 15 minutes. Makes 24.

SPOON DROP BISCUITS

2 cups flour

3 tablespoons baking powder

3¹/₂ tablespoons shortening

1 cup milk

Combine dry ingredients, cut in shortening. Add milk, mix well. Drop by spoonfuls onto cookie sheet and bake at 425 degrees for 15 minutes.

LILLIE LANGTRY, *an English actress known as Jersey Lily because she was born on the island of Jersey, was more noted for her beauty, her role in society, and her affair with Edward VII than as an actress. The notorious western American character, Judge Roy Bean, was infatuated with her and named his saloon in Texas the Jersey Lilly.*

BLUE CHEESE BISCUIT BITES

1 (10 count) can refrigerated biscuits

¼ cup butter or margarine

3 tablespoons crumbled blue cheese

Quarter biscuits; arrange in 8 x 1½ inch round baking dishes. Melt butter and cheese together. Drizzle over biscuits. Bake at 400 degrees until brown — 12 to 15 minutes.

AFTERNOON TEA BISCUITS

1 cup flour

1 (3 ounce) package cream cheese

½ teaspoon salt

½ cup butter

Mix flour, cream cheese, salt, and butter with a fork. Roll to ¼ inch thickness. Cut with small biscuit cutter. Bake at 425 degrees on an ungreased cookie sheet for 12 to 15 minutes.

CHEDDAR CHEESE DROP BISCUITS

2 cups Bisquick®

1 cup grated Cheddar cheese

⅛ teaspoon cayenne pepper

1 cup milk

In a large bowl, put Bisquick®, cheese, and cayenne and mix well. Add milk and mix. Drop by tablespoon onto a lightly greased baking sheet 1 inch apart. Bake at 425 degrees for 12 to 14 minutes. Makes 4 to 6 servings.

EDNA ST. VINCENT MILLAY was a leading American poet of the first half of the 20th century, and a symbol of life in the early 1920's in Greenwich Village. She wrote the title poem for her first volume, Renascence, when she was 19.

WHIPPED CREAM BISCUITS

2 cups flour

3 teaspoons baking powder

¾ teaspoon salt

1 cup whipping cream, whipped

Sift dry ingredients and add to whipped cream. Roll ½ inch thick and cut with biscuit cutter. Bake at 350 degrees for 15 minutes. Makes 18.

GARLIC PARMESAN BREAD

1 loaf frozen bread dough, thawed

6 tablespoons grated Parmesan cheese

1 teaspoon garlic powder

½ cup margarine

Cut dough into 16 pieces; shape into balls. Place on floured surface. Cover and let rise in warm place for 10 minutes. In a bowl, stir cheese and garlic powder into margarine, and mix well. Roll balls into margarine mixture. Arrange loosely in a 9-inch baking pan. Cover and let rise until doubled. Bake at 375 degrees for 10 to 15 minutes or until golden brown.

Although she was involved in many humanitarian projects, JANE ADDAMS (1860–1935) is most remembered for her first and most beloved project, the founding of Hull House. There the tired, the poor, and the wretched refuse of Chicago's teeming factories were made to feel welcome. She was also one of the founders of the American Civil Liberties Union.

QUICKIE BEER BREAD

3 cups self-rising flour

2 tablespoons sugar

1 (12 ounce) can beer

In bowl mix flour, sugar and beer. Blend with mixer. Pour into greased loaf pan. Bake 55 minutes at 350 degrees. Brush top with soft butter, then bake 5 more minutes.

GREEN CHILE BREAD

1 (8 ounce) jar cheese spread

1 (4 ounce) can chopped green chiles, drained

1 pound loaf Italian bread

Mix cheese spread and chiles. Cut loaf diagonally into 1 inch slices to within ½ inch of bottom. Spread both sides of each slice with cheese mixture. Place loaf on 18 x 18 inch piece of aluminum foil. Bring foil up around loaf, pressing against sides and leaving top uncovered. Bake 20 minutes at 350 degrees. Makes 4 to 6 servings.

BUSY-DAY POPOVERS

1 cup flour

½ teaspoon salt

1 cup milk

2 eggs

Measure flour by dip level pour method. Beat all ingredients together until smooth. Pour into well greased muffin cups ¾ full. Bake at 425 degrees for 40 minutes or until golden brown.

ETHEL MERMAN reigned as "Queen of Broadway" for three decades. She was known for her "wake 'em up in the last row" voice. She debuted on Broadway in Crazy Girl, *in 1930. Other Broadway musicals in which she starred include* Anything Goes, Annie Get Your Gun, Call Me Madam, Gypsy, *and* Hello, Dolly!. *She was in several movie musicals, including* There's No Business Like Show Business.

MAYONNAISE BREAD PUFFS

2 cups all-purpose flour

2 teaspoons baking powder

½ cup mayonnaise

¾ cup milk

Combine flour, baking powder and ½ teaspoon salt in a small mixing bowl. Add mayonnaise and milk, stirring until ingredients are moistened. Spoon into lightly greased muffin pan, filling ¾ full. Bake at 450 degrees for 10 to 12 minutes. Makes 8 muffins.

FRIED CORNBREAD

1½ cups white cornmeal

½ tablespoon salt

¾ cup boiling water

Bacon grease

Mix cornmeal and salt; beating constantly, slowly pour into boiling water. Drop by tablespoon into hot grease, turn once. Cook until golden brown. Makes 4 to 6 servings.

SOUR CREAM CORNBREAD

1 cup self-rising cornmeal

3 eggs

1 cup cream-style corn

1 cup sour cream

Combine all ingredients, mix well. Pour into greased pan. Bake at 400 degrees for30 to 40 minutes. Makes 4 to 6 servings.

On July 11, 1992, **TRACY AUSTIN** *(born in 1962) became the youngest person ever inducted into the International Tennis Hall of Fame in Newport, Rhode Island. She became the youngest U.S. Open champion in 1979, and was rated the number one woman player in 1980. She broke her leg in an auto accident in 1989 and her career came to an early end.*

GENE'S CORNBREAD

1 egg

1½ cups milk

1 stick margarine

1½ cups self-rising cornmeal

Mix egg and milk together. Melt margarine in 9 to 10 inch cast iron skillet in oven while preheating oven to 425 degrees. Pour one half melted margarine into milk and egg mixture. Return skillet to oven and get margarine hot. Add cornmeal to milk, egg and margarine. Mix well. Add more milk if needed. Pour into hot skillet with hot margarine. When margarine comes up sides of skillet, spoon over top of mixture. Bake 30 minutes or until golden brown. Makes 6 servings.

THE BEST FRIED CORNBREAD

2 cups cornmeal

2 eggs

2 cups milk

½ cup butter, melted

Place cornmeal in bowl. Add eggs, milk, and butter. Mix well. Drop mixture in greased skillet or griddle, like pancakes. Brown both sides.

Her appearance on the cover of Elle *led to the film debut of* **BRIGITTE BARDOT,** *a Parisian ballet student and model. Her reputation as a sex kitten was established in* And God Created Woman *in 1956. She became an international symbol of a new female permissiveness that was reinforced by her much publicized off-screen love life. After many movies she retired and campaigned for animal rights, founding the Foundation for the Protection of Distressed Animals in 1976.*

CRUMBLE SAUSAGE CORNBREAD

1 pound pork sausage

2 cups self-rising cornmeal

1½ cups milk

2 eggs

Crumble sausage in skillet and lightly brown. Drain excess fat and allow meat to cool. Mix cornmeal, milk, and eggs together. Beat well. Stir in sausage. Pour into greased 9 inch pan (or skillet). Bake at 400 degrees for 35 minutes.

DOWN SOUTH CORN CAKES

1 teaspoon salt

1 pint boiling water

1¼ cups cornmeal

Shortening

Add salt to boiling water. Gradually sift in cornmeal. Set in refrigerator for 20 minutes or until chilled and firm. Shape into balls about 1 inch in diameter and fry in 1 inch of shortening at 350 degrees. Cook until golden brown. Drain on absorbent paper and serve hot! Makes 18 corn cakes.

HUSH PUPPIES

2¼ cups self-rising cornmeal

3 tablespoons self-rising flour

1 egg

1 cup milk

Combine cornmeal, and flour. Add egg and gradually beat in milk. Drop from spoon into hot oil. Fry until golden brown, drain on paper towels.

CHARLOTTE BRONTE and EMILY BRONTE, the *Bronte sisters, remain two of the most read and admired writers of the nineteenth century. Emily is best known for* Wuthering Heights (*a commercial failure when first written*) *and Charlotte for* Jane Eyre.

QUICK HUSH PUPPIES

1 cup yellow cornmeal

¾ teaspoon baking powder

¼ cup milk

1 egg

Mix cornmeal and baking powder. Add milk and egg. Mix well. Drop batter by teaspoons into hot oil and cook for 3 to 5 minutes. Drain on paper towel.

QUICK ROLLS

1 (8 ounce) package brown and serve rolls

2 tablespoons margarine or butter, softened

¼ teaspoon onion salt

¼ teaspoon sesame seeds

Place rolls on ungreased cookie sheet, spread butter on rolls, sprinkle with onion salt and sesame seeds. Bake as directed on package. Makes 4 to 6 servings.

QUICK-AS-A-WINK CHEESE BREAD

1 egg

1½ cups milk

3¾ cups Bisquick®

¾ cups Cheddar cheese

Beat egg and add milk. Stir in Bisquick® and cheese. Beat until well blended. Pour into greased loaf pan. Bake at 350 degrees for 1 hour.

NELLIE BLY (Elizabeth Cochrane Seaman) was an American journalist whose well planned feats attracted wide attention. She was best known for her attempt to beat the fictional Phineas Phog's trip "Around the World in Eighty Days." She did it in 1889–90 in seventy two days.

CARAWAY-CHEESE ROLLS

1 (4 ounce) container whipped cream cheese with pimientos

1 teaspoon caraway seeds

1 teaspoon finely chopped green onion with top

8 to 10 hard rolls

Mix cream cheese, caraway seeds and green onion. Split each roll lengthwise, cutting to, but not through, opposite side of roll. Spread rolls with cream cheese mixture. Wrap rolls loosely in heavy-duty foil. Bake at 375 degrees for 15 minutes.

CRISS-CROSS DINNER ROLLS

2 cups self-rising flour

1 cup milk

½ cup mayonnaise

Mix all ingredients in bowl. Mix well. Drop 1 tablespoon dough on floured board. Roll into a ball and place on greased cookie sheet. With knife, criss-cross top of ball. Bake at 425 degrees for 10 minutes. Makes 16 rolls.

DORIS DAY begun singing on the radio. In 1940 she joined Les Brown's band and made several popular recordings, including "Sentimental Journey." As a movie actress she came to epitomize the ideal American woman of the 1950's. She is still seen on television in reruns of the 1960's sophisticated sex comedies, probably with Rock Hudson. After her acting career she focused her efforts on proper treatment of animals.

Sugar and Spice

Famous
First Women

41. ANNETTE ABBOTT ADAMS served in the Northern California District from July 25, 1918, to June 26, 1920, as the first woman district attorney of the United States.

42. SARAH G. BAGLEY became the first woman telegrapher on February 21, 1846, when the New York and Boston Magnetic Telegraph Association opened the line between Boston and Lowell, Massachusetts.

43. The first offspring of a president born in the White House was ESTHER CLEVELAND, born September 5, 1893, the second child of President Grover Cleveland.

44. COUNTESS GERALDINE APPONIJI of Hungary married King Zog of Albania on April 27, 1938, and was the first woman of American descent to become a queen.

45. ROBERTA A. KNAKUS underwent 14 months of on-the-job training at Philadelphia Electric Company's Peach Bottom Atomic power plant. On February 12, 1976, the graduate of Rensselar Polytechnic Institute was licensed by the Nuclear Regulatory Commission and became the first licensed woman operator at a commercial nuclear power plant.

46. Benjamin Franklin's sister-in-law, ANN FRANKLIN, became the first woman newspaper editor when she took charge of the Newport Mercury, Newport, Rhode Island, upon the death of her son on August 22, 1762. She edited the paper until her death on April 16, 1763.

47. BELLE MARTELL became the first licensed woman prize fight referee when California issued her a license on April 30, 1940. Her first assignment was a complete show of eight bouts in San Bernardino on May 2, 1940. She retired the following month after an assignment in Los Angeles.

AUTHOR'S NOTE: We recommend using ready made crusts. In some cases this adds a fifth or sixth ingredient.

FRESH BLUEBERRY PIE

4 cups fresh blueberries

3 tablespoons honey

1½ tablespoons cornstarch

1 (9 inch) pie crust, baked

In saucepan, combine 2 cups of the berries with honey and cornstarch. Simmer over low heat for 10 minutes, stirring occasionally until berries are soft. Remove from heat and stir in remaining raw blueberries. Stir to cool. Spoon into crust and chill.

SWEET CHERRY PIE

3 cups canned sweet cherries

¼ cup sugar

2½ tablespoons quick-cooking tapioca

2 teaspoons butter

2 (8 inch) pie crust, unbaked

Drain cherries, saving ½ cup of juice. Mix juice, sugar, and tapioca in a bowl. Add cherries and toss well. Pour into 8 inch unbaked pie crust and dot with butter. Cover top with 8 inch unbaked pie crust. Crimp the edges and cut several vents in top. Bake at 425 degrees for 10 minutes then reduce heat to 350 degrees. Bake 30 to 40 minutes more.

PRINCESS DIANA was greatly admired and probably the most photographed woman in the world, and she has acquired cult status after her death in an auto accident. She had survived the problems and scandals of her 1981 marriage and 1996 divorce from Prince Charles—from whom she received a $26 million settlement. Her many charity efforts included an auction of her clothes which raised $3.25 million for AIDS and breast cancer research. She was tireless in her activities against land mines.

CREAMY BERRY PIE

1 (3 ounce) package cream cheese, softened

1 (9 inch) graham cracker crust

4 cups strawberries

½ cup blueberries

1 (14 ounce) carton strawberry glaze

Beat cream cheese with electric mixer, until smooth. Spread on bottom of 9 inch graham cracker crust. Gently fold strawberries and blueberries into glaze. Spoon over cream cheese. Chill until set.

CHOCOLATE SUNDAY PIE

1 pint chocolate ice cream, softened

1 (9 inch) graham cracker crust

1½ pints vanilla ice cream

½ cup hot fudge sauce

Spread softened chocolate ice cream in 9 inch graham cracker pie crust. Scoop ice cream balls from vanilla ice cream and arrange close together on top of pie. Return to freezer for 1 hour or until ready to serve. Just before serving, drizzle warm fudge sauce over pie.

JACQUELINE KENNEDY ONASSIS, wife of the 35th President of the United States, John F. Kennedy, was noted for her style and elegance. As the cultured and sophisticated first lady she helped set the social tone for the Kennedy administration. Her pillbox hat and Oleg Cassini creations set fashion styles. Her husband's assassination and her remarriage to Aristotle Onassis, one of the wealthiest men in the world, fueled an almost insatiable interest in her by the media and the public.

CHOCOLATE CHERRY PIE

1 (4 serving) box instant chocolate pudding

1 (9 inch) graham cracker crust

1 (8 ounce) tub frozen whipped topping

1 (15 ounce) can cherry pie filling

Prepare chocolate pudding as directed on box. Layer pudding in pie crust and add whipped topping. Pour cherry pie filling on top. Refrigerate until set.

EMERGENCY CHOCOLATE PIE

2 cups vanilla ice cream

1 cup milk

1 (4 serving) box instant chocolate pudding

1 (8 inch) graham cracker crust

Combine ice cream, milk, and pudding mix. Beat until smooth. Spoon into pie crust. Refrigerate until firm. May be garnished with whipped topping.

PINK LEMONADE PIE

1 (8 ounce) package cream cheese

1 (14 ounce) can sweetened condensed milk

1 (6 ounce) can pink lemonade

1 (8 ounce) tub frozen whipped topping

1 (8 inch) graham cracker crust

Put cream cheese, milk, and pink lemonade in blender. Blend well and fold in whipped topping. Pour into pie crust.

BETTE DAVIS (1908-1989) rose above the criticism that she had no sex appeal to become one of American movies' greatest actresses. Her career spanned over 60 years, during which she made about 100 movies. Known for her strong, volatile temperament, she waged some spectacular legal battles with Warner Brothers over scripts. She was nominated 10 times for Academy Awards, winning for Dangerous *in 1935 and* Jezebel *in 1938. She also won an Emmy in 1979 for her performance in* Strangers.

LEMONADE PIE

1 (6 ounce) can frozen lemonade

1 (14 ounce) can sweetened condensed milk

1 (8 ounce) tub frozen whipped topping

1 (8 inch) graham cracker crust

Mix all ingredients together and pour into crust. Chill and serve. **Alternate:** Substitute 1 pint vanilla ice cream (softened) for condensed milk.

LEMON SLICED PIE

2 large lemons

2 cups sugar

4 eggs, beaten

2 (8 inch) pie crusts, unbaked

Slice lemons thinly, leaving the rinds on, remove seeds. In a bowl, mix slices with sugar and let stand overnight. Add beaten eggs to mixture and mix. Pour into pastry lined pan and cover with top crust. Crimp and cut several vents in top. Bake at 450 degrees for 15 minutes. Reduce heat to 375 degrees and bake for 20 minutes.

GOLDEN LEMON PIE

3 eggs

1 cup sugar

1½ cups whipping cream

Juice of 2 large lemons

1 (9 inch) pie crust, unbaked

Beat eggs until frothy. Beat in sugar and add cream. Stir in lemon juice. Pour into 9 inch unbaked pie crust. Bake at 375 degrees until top is golden brown, about 20 minutes.

AGATHA CHRISTIE *created in her mystery stories two unusual detectives, Miss Jane Marple, a quiet spinster, and Hercule Poirot, a fussy Belgian private eye. Her books sold several hundred million copies and her play,* The Mousetrap, *opened in London November 25, 1952, and will probably run forever.*

LIME PIE

2 (8 ounce) packages cream cheese

1 teaspoon grated lime peel

½ cup lime juice

1 (12 ounce) can sweetened condensed milk

Pretzel Crust (see page 181)

In large bowl, put cream cheese, lime peel, lime juice and condensed milk. With mixer, mix until smooth. Pour into pretzel crust. Cover and freeze, 6 hours.

FESTIVE MINCE PIE

1 cup whipped cream

1 (28 ounce) jar mincemeat

3 tablespoons brown sugar

2 tablespoons flour

¾ cup pecan halves

2 (8 inch) pie crusts, unbaked

Fold whipped cream into mincemeat and spread in pastry-lined pie pan. Combine brown sugar and flour. Sprinkle over mincemeat. Arrange pecan halves on top of mixture. Cover with top crust, which has about ten one inch slits cut in it. Seal well by folding top crust under bottom crust and flute. Bake at 425 degrees for 40 to 45 minutes.

KATHERINE DUNHAM, well known for her influential work in modern dance, is also a political activist, teacher, and international artistic advisor to heads of state. She is a recognized authority on the dances and rituals of the black peoples of tropical America, including the West Indies. In 1963 she became the first black choreographer at the Metropolitan Opera in New York City with their production of Aida. Her work later in life has centered on bringing art to disadvantaged urban youth through the Performing Arts Training Center in East St. Louis, Illinois.

EASY PEACH PIE

1 cup sugar

2 tablespoons flour

1 (29 ounce) can sliced peaches, drained

2 (9 inch) pie crusts, unbaked

Put ½ cup sugar and 1 tablespoon flour in bottom of 9-inch unbaked pie crust. Place peaches on top of flour and sugar. Put the other ½ cup of sugar and 1 tablespoon of flour on top of peaches; use another pie crust for top crust. Seal, cut slits on top. Bake at 425 degrees for 10 minutes. Reduce heat to 350 degrees for 30 minutes.

FRESH PEACH PIE

7 peaches, peeled and sliced

¼ cup sugar

2 tablespoons cornstarch

2 tablespoons margarine

1 (9 inch) pie crust, baked

Place all ingredients in pan and cook over medium heat until thick and clear. Pour into 9 inch baked pie crust. Refrigerate.

QUICK RAISIN PIE

1 cup whipping cream

1 cup sugar

1 cup raisins

1 teaspoon cinnamon

1 (9 inch) pie crust, baked

In saucepan, add cream, sugar, raisins and cinnamon. Cook over low heat. Cook until thick. Pour into 9-inch baked pie crust.

Few millionaires have spent their fortunes as wisely and as well as Baroness **ANGELA BURDETT-COUTTS,** *the richest heiress in Victorian England. Whenever there came a legitimate cry for help, she opened her purse. She was the first woman to receive the keys to the cities of London and Edinburg as well as the Turkish order of Medjidie. She was known throughout the British Isles as "Queen of the Poor."*

TWO PINEAPPLE PIES

1 (12 ounce) tub frozen whipped
  topping, thawed

1 (14 ounce) can sweetened condensed
  milk

1 (8¼ ounce) can crushed pineapple,
  undrained

¼ cup lemon juice

2 (8 or 9 inch) pie crusts, baked

Mix whipped topping, milk, pineapple, and
lemon juice. Mix well. Pour into 2 baked 8 or 9
inch pie crusts. Chill. Can be frozen.

PINEAPPLE PIE

2 (20 ounce) cans crushed pineapple,
  drained, reserve liquid

½ cup sugar

3 tablespoons flour

1 tablespoon butter

2 (9 inch) pie crusts

Combine pineapple, sugar, and flour, mix well.
Pour into 9-inch pie crust. Pour ¾ cup pineapple liquid over pie, dot with butter. Put on top
crust and seal edges, make a few small slits on
top crust. Bake at 375 degrees for 30 to 35 minutes.

*CATHERINE
THE GREAT
(1729–1796) is
remembered by
popular history for
her many lovers
and libidinous
lifestyle.
Catherine II,
empress of Russia,
acquired her title
of the Great by
accomplishments
in foreign affairs,
bringing Russia
from a relatively
backward country
into a powerful
nation.*

HOLIDAY PUMPKIN PIE

1 (16 ounce) can pumpkin

1 (14 ounce) can sweetened condensed milk

2 eggs

1¼ teaspoons pumpkin pie spice

1 (9 inch) pie crust, unbaked

Combine all ingredients and mix well. Pour into unbaked 9 inch pie crust. Bake at 400 degrees for 15 minutes. Reduce heat to 350 degrees and bake for 35 to 40 minutes.

STRAWBERRY VANILLA PIE

2 cups fresh or frozen strawberries

1 cup sugar

1 (4 serving) box strawberry-flavored gelatin

1 pint vanilla ice cream

1 (9 inch) pie crust, baked

Whipped cream

Combine strawberries and sugar. Let stand for 10 minutes. Drain off liquid and measure. Add water to make 1 cup. Pour liquid into saucepan and heat to boiling and pour over gelatin. Stir until dissolved. Add ice cream and stir until melted. Add berries and mix. Pour into 9 inch baked pie crust. Chill. Top with whipped cream.

One of the outstanding vocal talents of the past century, **MARIAN ANDERSON,** *was the first African-American to become a permanent member of the Metropolitan Opera Company. When the D.A.R. forbade her to sing at Constitution Hall, Eleanor Roosevelt resigned in protest and arranged for her to sing at the Lincoln Memorial where she drew 85,000 people.*

JUST MINUTES STRAWBERRY PIE

1 (4 serving) box strawberry-flavored gelatin

1 cup boiling water

1 (16 ounce) package frozen sweetened, sliced strawberries, thawed

1 (8 inch) pie crust, baked

Whipped cream

Dissolve gelatin in water. Add thawed frozen strawberries. When partially set, pour into cooled pie crust. Chill until completely set. Garnish with whipped cream.

WHAT-A-DREAM PIE

1 pint vanilla ice cream, softened

1½ cups malted milk balls, crushed

1 (9 inch) graham cracker crust

⅓ cup marshmallow topping

1 (8 ounce) tub frozen whipped topping, softened

Combine ice cream with ½ cup crushed malted milk balls. Spread mixture into graham cracker crust. Freeze. Blend marshmallow topping with ¾ cup crushed malted milk balls. Fold into whipped topping and spread over frozen ice cream layer. Freeze. Top with remaining ¼ cup crushed malted milk balls.

HARRIET BEECHER STOWE's *novel of slavery,* Uncle Tom's Cabin, *in 1852, crystallized the abolitionist sentiments of the North and gave the moral purpose to the Civil War. Few works of fiction have ever had such an influence. Twenty thousand copies were sold in three weeks and an estimated 3,000,000 copies were eventually sold in the United States alone.*

CHERRY CHEESECAKE

1 (8 ounce) package cream cheese, softened

1 (14 ounce) can sweetened condensed milk

1/3 cup lemon juice

1 (9 inch) graham cracker crust

1 (15 ounce) can cherry pie filling

Mix cream cheese, milk, and lemon juice. Pour into a 9 inch graham cracker crust. Top with cherry pie filling. Chill.

MERINGUE

4 egg whites

1/2 teaspoon cream of tartar

8 tablespoons sugar

Beat egg whites and cream of tartar until frothy. Add sugar, 1 tablespoon at a time and beat until egg whites stand in a stiff peak. Top pie. Bake at 350 degrees for 8 to 10 minutes

AMISH PIE DOUGH

1½ cups flour

2 tablespoons sugar

2 tablespoons milk

1/2 cup salad oil

Mix all ingredients in an 8 or 9 inch pie pan and press on bottom and sides. Bake at 350 degrees for 20 minutes.

EDITH WILSON, a descendant of Pocahontas, was the second wife of President Woodrow Wilson and has been referred to as our first woman president. When her husband had a serious stroke, she decided he could still accomplish more with a maimed body than people with healthy bodies. President's doctors agreed that his mind was clear, so anyone wanting to see him had to come through her. She decided which matters were important enough for his attention. She maintained that she never made a decision regarding the disposition of public affairs.

BAKED PIE CRUST

1 cup flour

3 tablespoons sugar

½ cup butter or margarine, softened

Mix all ingredients and press in 8 or 9 inch pie pan. Bake at 350 degrees until edges begin to brown. Cool; fill with any filling.

HOT WATER PIE CRUST

1 cup boiling water

⅔ cup shortening

2 cups flour

¾ teaspoon salt

Pour hot water over shortening; beat until creamy. Cool. Add flour, sifted with salt. Mix to soft dough. Wrap in waxed paper and chill thoroughly before rolling. Makes 2-8 inch pie crust.

PRETZEL CRUST

1¼ cups crushed pretzels

½ cup butter or margarine, melted

¼ cup sugar

Mix all ingredients. Press mixture firmly against bottom and sides of 9-inch pie plate. Refrigerate until firm.

ELEANOR ROOSEVELT, America's 32nd first lady, was the first president's wife to pursue an independent career of public service and to speak out on controversial issues. New York Times *editorial: "No first lady could touch her for causes espoused, opinions expressed, words printed, precedents shattered, honors conferred, degrees garnered."*

NUT CRUST

1/2 cup butter or margarine

1 cup flour

1/2 cup crushed nuts

Cut butter into flour; add nuts. Press in 9-inch pie pan and bake at 350 degrees for 20 minutes. Cool.

COCOA COOKIE CRUST

3/4 cup flour

1/2 cup butter, softened

1/4 cup confectioners' sugar

2 tablespoons baking cocoa

Mix all ingredients until soft dough forms. Press mixture evenly in 8 or 9 inch pie pan. Bake at 350 degrees for 10-15 minutes or until light brown.

GRAHAM CRACKER CRUST

1 1/2 cups crushed graham crackers

1/3 cup sugar

1/2 cup butter or margarine, melted

Combine crumbs with sugar and blend with melted butter. Press firmly onto bottom and sides of a 9-inch pie pan. Chill 1 hour or bake at 350 degrees for 10 minutes to set crust.

JANE TODD CRAWFORD rode 60 rugged miles in three days on horseback from her home in Green County to Danville, Kentucky. There, on December 12, 1809, Dr. Ephriam McDowell removed from her a 22 1/2 pound ovarian tumor, the first successful operation of its kind. The 25 minute surgery was done with no anesthesia. Less than three weeks later she rode the same horse back home. She died 32 years later at the age of 78.

SUNNY DELIGHT CAKE

1 box pineapple cake mix

4 eggs

½ cup cooking oil

1 (11 ounce) can mandarin oranges with juice

Combine cake mix, eggs, oil, and oranges. Beat 4 minutes at medium speed. Pour into three greased and floured 8 inch round cake pans. Bake at 350 degrees for 30 to 35 minutes.

Sunny Delight Frosting:

1 (4 serving) box instant pineapple cream pudding

1 (20 ounce) can crushed pineapple, drained

1 (8 ounce) tub frozen whipped topping, softened

Pour dry pudding over pineapple. Let set for 20 minutes. Mix and fold in whipped topping. Frost cake.

GIVE-ME-A-BREAK PINEAPPLE CAKE

1 box yellow cake mix

1 (22 ounce) can crushed pineapple

2 (4 serving) boxes instant vanilla pudding

3 cups milk

Prepare and bake cake according to package directions for 13 x 9 inch baking pan. Pierce cake with fork at frequent intervals and top with pineapple and juice. Prepare pudding according to directions using milk. Spread on top of pineapple. Top with whipped topping (optional).

*In a letter to her husband, President John Adams in 1774, **ABIGAIL ADAMS** wrote: "Whilst you are proclaiming peace and goodwill to men, emancipating all nations, you insist on retaining absolute power over wives … Remember the ladies and be more generous and favorable to them than your ancestors … Do not put such unlimited power in the hands of husbands … If particular care and attention is not paid to the ladies, we are determined to foment a rebellion and will not hold ourselves bound by any laws in which we have no voice or representation."*

PEACHY NUT CAKE

1 (28 ounce) can peaches

1 box butter pecan cake mix

¾ cup butter

½ cup chopped nuts

Place peaches in 13 x 8 x2 pan. Sprinkle cake mix on peaches evenly. Pour melted butter over mix. Add nuts and bake at 325 degrees for 55 minutes.

MANDARIN ORANGE PARTY CAKE

1 box yellow butter cake mix

4 eggs

½ cup oil

1 (11 ounce) can mandarin oranges, undrained

Combine cake mix, eggs, oil, and mandarin oranges. Mix well. Pour batter into 4 prepared 8 inch cake pans. Bake at 325 degrees for 30 minutes, two layers at a time.

SUGAR AND SPICE CAKE

1 box spice cake mix

½ cup confectioners' sugar

1 teaspoon cinnamon

½ cup chopped nuts

Mix spice cake per directions on box. Pour cake in greased cake pan. Sprinkle with sugar, cinnamon, and nuts over top. Bake at 350 degrees for 40 to 45 minutes.

ROSA PARKS has been called the first lady of civil rights. She refused to give up her seat on a bus to a white person in December, 1955, in Montgomery, Alabama. She was arrested, jailed and released on $100 bail. She refused to pay the $14 fine, and Martin Luther King, Jr., led a 381 day boycott of the Montgomery buses. This catalyzed the civil rights movement and was the model for the non-violent sit-ins and boycotts that led the courts to strike down segregation laws.

ICE CREAM CONE CAKES

1 box chocolate or yellow cake mix

24 flat-bottom ice cream cones
    frosting

½ cup sprinkles

Prepare cake mix as directed on package. Spoon about ¼ cup batter into each cone. Set cones on baking sheet. Bake at 350 degrees for 25 minutes. Cool on rack. Spoon frosting over cakes. Garnish with sprinkles, if desired. Kids will love these cupcakes.

CABIN FEVER CHOCOLATE CAKE

1 (4 serving) box instant chocolate
    pudding

1 box devil's food cake mix

½ cup chopped nuts

1 (6 ounce) package chocolate chips

Preheat oven to 350°. In a medium bowl, prepare pudding according to package directions. Add cake mix, nuts and chips and mix well. Pour into a greased, 13 x 9 inch baking pan. Bake at 350° for 30 minutes until a toothpick inserted in center of cake comes out clean.

Cabin Fever Frosting:

⅓ cup milk

1 cup sugar

5 tablespoons butter or margarine

1 (6 ounce) package milk chocolate chips

Combine all ingredients in saucepan. Bring to a boil. Cook 1 minute. Cool. Spread over cooled cake.

*In 1991, **JUDIT POLGAR,** of Hungary became the youngest chess player to ever achieve the rank of grand master. The 15 year old was one month younger than former world champion, Bobby Fischer, when he achieved the ranking. She is only the fourth woman to ever become a grand master. She also has three expert chess playing sisters.*

GENE'S DUMP CAKE

1 (15¼ ounce) can cherry pie filling

1 (15¼ ounce) can crushed pineapple, undrained

1 box yellow cake mix

1½ cups margarine, melted

Mix cherry pie filling and pineapple. Put in baking dish. Sprinkle dry cake mix over filling, pour margarine over dry cake mix. Bake at 350 degrees for 35 minutes.

SUNSHINE CAKE

1 box yellow cake mix

2 (11 ounce) cans mandarin oranges, undrained

3 eggs

Mix all ingredients together. Pour into 13 x 9 inch cake pan. Bake at 350 degrees for 35 to 40 minutes.

Sunshine Frosting:

2 tablespoons butter, softened

2 cups sugar

3 tablespoons milk

¼ teaspoon orange extract

Put butter in bowl and add sugar gradually, beating well. Thin with milk until right consistency to spread. Add orange extract. Mix well.

*ELIZABETH TAYLOR was the first actress to earn $1 million for a movie. Once considered our most beautiful star, she won two Oscars (*Butterfield 8 *and* Who's Afraid of Virginia Wolfe). *She has survived weight gains and losses, eight marriages, 40 surgeries, addictions to painkillers and alcohol, scandals, tragedies, and constant media and public curiosity, to be our longest reigning glamour queen.*

MIRACLE WHIP® CHOCOLATE CAKE

1 cup Miracle Whip®

3 eggs

1 box devils' food cake mix

1⅓ cups water

Combine all ingredients and mix well. Pour into greased 13 x 9 inch cake pan. Bake at 350 degrees for 35 to 40 minutes.

QUICK-STEP SHORTCAKE

¾ cup whipping cream

2 cups Bisquick®

2 tablespoons sugar

Add cream to Bisquick and sugar. Mix thoroughly. Knead 10 times on flour surface. Pat or roll dough to half the thickness desired. Cut into individual shortcakes with cutter. Bake at 450 degrees for 10 to 15 minutes. Makes 6.

Strawberries For Shortcake:

1 quart fresh strawberries

1 cup sugar

Wash, hull, and cut up strawberries. Sprinkle with sugar and let stand 1 hour.

HARRIET ROSS TUBMAN was an escaped slave who had a United States postage stamp issued in her honor in 1977. As a "conductor" of the Underground Railroad that guided slaves to safety, she was personally responsible for the manumission of 300 black slaves. She became a legend in the North, and in the South a $40,000 reward was offered for her capture.

PINEAPPLE UPSIDE DOWN CAKE

¼ cup butter

½ cup packed brown sugar

7 pineapple slices, save juice

1 box yellow cake mix

Melt butter, brown sugar, and 2 tablespoons of pineapple juice in skillet. Remove from heat and arrange pineapple in 13 x 9 inch baking pan. Pour mixture over pineapple. Prepare cake batter as described on cake box. Pour over mixture. Bake at 350 degrees for 40 to 50 minutes.

FRUIT COCKTAIL CAKE

1 (17 ounce) can fruit cocktail with juice

1 box yellow cake mix

1¼ cups flaked coconut

2 eggs

Mix all ingredients and beat with mixer for 2 minutes. Pour into a greased 9 x 13 inch pan. Bake at 350 degrees for 40 to 45 minutes.

Cocktail Frosting:

1 cup packed brown sugar

¼ cup milk

1 stick butter

1 cup flaked coconut

In a saucepan add brown sugar, milk, and butter. Cook over medium heat for 5 minutes. Add coconut and cool until warm. Pour over cake.

MARY BALL WASHINGTON lived long enough to see her son, George, elected President of the United States, but she did not attend his inauguration. Her son's activities during the Revolutionary War had made her quite angry. He should have been home taking care of his mother instead of off playing general. At considerable personal sacrifice he provided for her financial needs, but she complained to the Virginia Legislature about, her lack of funds— embarrassing her son.

BUTTER FROSTING

4 tablespoons butter

2 cups confectioners' sugar

3 tablespoons milk

1 teaspoon vanilla

Cream butter, add vanilla and 1 cup sugar gradually, blending after each addition. Add remaining sugar, alternately with milk until thick enough to spread.

HOMEMADE CARAMEL ICING

1 cup packed brown sugar

4 tablespoons butter

¼ cup milk

1½ cups confectioners' sugar

In saucepan, add brown sugar, butter, and milk. Boil 2 minutes. Cool to lukewarm. Add confectioners' sugar and beat until smooth.

OLD TIME CARAMEL FROSTING

1 (12 ounce) can evaporated milk

1 (16 ounce) box brown sugar

3 tablespoons butter

1 teaspoon vanilla

Mix milk and sugar well. Bring to a boil and continue to boil for 3 minutes. Remove from heat. Add butter and vanilla. Beat until cool.

BARBARA WALTERS' *position as one of the top television journalists has been earned by her many unique interviews. She has interviewed every U.S. President since Nixon; as well as a one-hour interview with Cuban president Fidel Castro; the first joint interview with Egyptian president, Anwar Sadat, and Israeli prime minister, Nehachem Begin in 1977. She spent 15 years on NBC's "Today Show" and was its first female co-host. In 1976 she was the first woman to co-host network news (ABC).*

CREAMY CHOCOLATE GLAZE

1 cup semisweet chocolate chips

2 tablespoons butter

3 tablespoons half and half

2 tablespoons light corn syrup

Heat chocolate chips and butter in saucepan over low heat, stirring frequently. Remove from heat, stir in half and half and corn syrup until smooth.

CHOCOLATE GLAZE

3 (1 ounce) squares semisweet chocolate

1 tablespoon margarine or butter

1 tablespoon corn syrup

In saucepan, heat chocolate, butter, and corn syrup on low heat, stirring constantly until chocolate is melted. Cool slightly.

EASY SPREAD CHOCOLATE ICING

1 ounce unsweetened chocolate

1 tablespoon butter

2 tablespoons boiling water

1 cup confectioners' sugar

Melt chocolate and butter over hot water. Remove from heat. Blend in water and sugar. Beat until smooth.

ELLEN LOUISE WILSON, first wife of President Woodrow Wilson, humorously insisting that her children not be born Yankees, went home to Georgia for the birth of her first two children. She studied art and her paintings compared favorably to professional art of the times. She had a studio with a skylight installed in the White House. She died of Bright's disease in 1914 and on the day before her death, she made her physician promise to tell her husband later that she hoped he would marry again.

BUSY DAY CHOCOLATE FROSTING

1 cup semisweet chocolate chips

¼ cup margarine or butter

½ cup sour cream

2½ cups confectioners' sugar

In a saucepan, melt chocolate and margarine over low heat, stirring frequently. Cool 5 minutes. Stir in sour cream. Gradually add confectioners' sugar, beating until smooth.

ONE MINUTE FUDGE FROSTING

½ cup cocoa

¼ cup milk

¼ cup butter

1 cup sugar

Combine all ingredients in saucepan. Cook over low heat and let boil for 1 minute. Remove from heat. Beat until icing is right consistency to spread.

MAPLE FROSTING

¼ cup packed brown sugar

2½ tablespoons water

1 egg white

¼ teaspoon maple extract

Cook sugar, water, and egg white in double boiler; beat constantly until frosting stands in peaks (about 7 minutes). Remove from heat. Add maple flavoring.

ELIZABETH DOLE was Secretary of Transportation in the Reagan administration (1981–83), Secretary of Labor for President Bush (1989–91), and President of the American Red Cross, (1991–99). She campaigned for her husband, Senator Robert Dole, in his 1996 presidential campaign, and was in an abbreviated campaign for the 2000 Republican nomination herself.

POWDERED SUGAR FROSTING

1 cup confectioners' sugar

¼ cup whipping cream

½ teaspoon vanilla extract

¼ teaspoon almond extract

In bowl, put confectioners' sugar, cream, vanilla and almond extracts. Mix until smooth.

ORANGE BUTTER FROSTING

2 tablespoons butter

2 cups confectioners' sugar

3 tablespoons milk

½ teaspoon orange extract

Work butter with spoon until very soft. Add sugar gradually, beating well, thinning with milk until right consistency to spread. Add orange extract. Mix well.

STRAWBERRY FROSTING

½ cup butter

1 pound confectioners' sugar

½ cup strawberries, thawed and mashed

Cream butter until smooth. Add sugar spoonfuls at a time. Cream well, adding strawberries as needed to mix sugar. Beat thoroughly.

CLEOPATRA (69-30 BC), queen of Egypt, was the last and most famous of the Macedonian dynasty of the Ptolemies. She bore a son by Julius Caesar who helped her regain her throne. After Caesar's assassination, she had a romance with Mark Anthony and had three children by him. Rome declared war on Anthony and Cleopatra, and Augustus defeated them. Mark Anthony, thinking Cleopatra dead, committed suicide. Then Cleopatra killed herself by having an asp bite her breast.

CREAMY ICING FOR COOKIES

1 cup sifted confectioners' sugar

¼ teaspoon salt

½ teaspoon vanilla

1½ teaspoons whipping cream

Blend sugar, salt, vanilla, and cream. If desired, tint with food coloring. Spreads easily on cookies.

COCONUT DROP COOKIES

7 ounces flaked coconut

⅔ cup all-purpose flour

1 cup chocolate syrup

2 teaspoons vanilla

Mix coconut and flour. Add syrup and vanilla. Mix well. Drop by teaspoons onto lightly greased cookie sheet. Bake at 375 degrees for 10 minutes. Makes 1½ dozen.

CANDY COOKIES

1 (12 ounce) can sweetened condensed milk

16 large marshmallows

1 (6 ounce) package chocolate chips

2 cups crushed graham crackers

Put milk, marshmallows, and chocolate chips into top of double boiler. Heat until mixture is melted. Remove from heat and add crushed graham crackers. Drop by teaspoonfuls onto wax papered cookie sheet. Allow to set overnight.

GYPSY ROSE LEE performed as a child act with her younger sister (who became actress JUNE HAVOC). Their mother was the stereotypical stage mother. The girls made as much as $1,200 per week in vaudeville. As a solo act, Gypsy became the best known stripper in burlesque in the 1930's. She helped lift her profession to the plane of respectability. Her very classy act led H.L. Mencken to coin the more dignified term for the profession, "ecdysiast." She also authored two murder mysteries and appeared in motion pictures. The story of her life is a favorite musical on stage and as a movie.

CHOCOLATE COOKIE NUGGETS

1 box deep chocolate cake mix

½ cup oil

¼ cup water

1 egg

In large mixing bowl, stir together all ingredients until well mixed. Drop from teaspoon onto an ungreased cookie sheet. Bake at 350 degrees for 10 to 12 minutes. Cool and sprinkle with confectioners' sugar (optional).

QUICK FIX COOKIES

1 box cake mix

2 eggs

⅓ cup oil

Mix all ingredients together. Drop by spoonfuls onto ungreased cookie sheet. Bake at 350 degrees for 10 to 12 minutes. Nuts, chocolate chips, raisins are optional.

PEANUT BUTTER KISSES

1 (18 ounce) jar peanut butter

1¼ cups sugar

2 eggs

1 (10 ounce) package Hershey Kisses®

Mix peanut butter, sugar and eggs. Roll into balls. Place onto ungreased cookie sheet and press slightly down on each ball. Bake at 350 degrees for 10-12 minutes, or until lightly browned. Place unwrapped Hershey Kiss® on top of each cookie. Cool.

*One of Hollywood's greatest fashion designers, during her 58 year career, **EDITH HEAD** worked on more than 1,000 films and received 35 Oscar nominations. In 1938 she had become the first woman to head the design department of a major movie studio-Paramount.*

EASY PEANUT BUTTER COOKIES

1 cup peanut butter

1 cup sugar

1 egg

½ teaspoon vanilla

Mix peanut butter and sugar and then stir in remaining ingredients. Shape in 1 inch balls and put onto ungreased cookie sheet. Press with fork to flatten slightly and bake at 350 degrees for 12 to 15 minutes. Makes 3 dozen.

QUICK PEANUT BUTTER COOKIES

1 (11 ounce) package piecrust mix

1 cup firmly packed brown sugar

½ cup creamy peanut butter

3 tablespoons water

Combine all ingredients and stir until thoroughly blended. Shape dough into 1 inch balls. Place 2 inches apart on ungreased cookie sheet. Flatten cookies to ¼ inch thickness with a fork, making a crisscross pattern. Bake at 375 degrees for 8 to 10 minutes. Cool. Makes 4½ dozen.

HOLIDAY FRUIT BALLS

½ cup dried prunes

½ cup dried apricots

½ cup raisins

½ cup chopped cashews

Rinse fruit and dry. Chop fruit into fine pieces. Mix fruit and cashews into small balls. Makes 1 – 1½ dozen.

RUTH BADER GINSBURG, the daughter of orthodox Jewish immigrants, was nominated as the second woman justice on the U. S. Supreme Court in 1993 by President Bill Clinton. As a lawyer she had argued six cases concerning women's rights before the Supreme Court and won five of them.

LOW CALORIE OATMEAL COOKIES

2 egg whites

⅓ cup maple syrup

1 cup rolled oats

½ cup flaked coconut

Beat egg whites until stiff. Combine syrup and oats in separate bowl and mix until well blended. Add coconut. Fold in egg whites. Drop by teaspoon onto lightly greased cookie sheet. Bake at 350 degrees for 15 minutes. Makes 30.

LEMON DELIGHT COOKIES

1 box lemon cake mix with pudding

2 cups frozen whipped topping, thawed

1 egg, slightly beaten

½ cup confectioners' sugar

Combine cake mix, whipped topping, and egg. Mix until moist. Form into small balls. Roll balls in sugar and place onto lightly greased cookie sheet. Bake at 350 degrees for 10 to 12 minutes. Cool.

FORGET ME COOKIES

2 egg whites, beaten stiff

¾ cup sugar

1 cup chocolate chips

1 cup chopped nuts

Mix all ingredients together. Drop by teaspoon onto greased cookie sheet. Place in preheated oven at 350 degrees. Turn off oven and let set overnight.

As owner of the Washington Post **KATHERINE GRAHAM** *became the most famous newspaper publisher and one of the most influential women in American. The Watergate investigation she financed and the stories she ran ultimately led to the resignation of President Richard Nixon.*

COCOA KISSES

3 egg whites

½ teaspoon cream of tartar

1 cup sugar

2 tablespoons unsweetened cocoa

Beat egg whites until foamy. Add cream of tartar; beat until soft peaks form. Gradually beat in sugar. Beat until stiff. Fold in cocoa. Drop batter by level teaspoonful onto oil-sprayed cookie sheets. Bake at 275 degrees for 18 to 20 minutes. Cool. Makes 8 dozen.

RICE CAKE S'MORES

1 plain rice cake

½ of (1 ounce) bar milk chocolate

12 miniature marshmallows

Put rice cake on plate, top with chocolate, then marshmallows. Microwave on high for 18 to 20 seconds. Let stand for 30 seconds. Makes 1.

COOKIE COCONUT BALLS

½ pound sweet cookies, crushed (any kind)

1½ tablespoons cocoa

1¼ cups flaked coconut, divided

1 (14 ounce) can sweetened condensed milk

Combine cookies, cocoa and 1 cup of coconut. Mix well with condensed milk. Roll into balls, the size of a walnut and roll in remaining coconut. Makes 1 dozen.

LADY GODIVA, wife of the Earl of Chester in eleventh century England, supposedly rode naked through the market place of Coventry in order to persuade her husband to reduce the taxes he had imposed. Legend says that she asked the townspeople to remain indoors, which they all did except for "Peeping Tom" who was struck blind.

SHORTBREAD COOKIES

1 cup unsalted butter

1 cup packed light brown sugar

1 teaspoon vanilla

2½ cups all-purpose flour, sifted

Beat the butter, brown sugar, and vanilla together until fluffy. Add flour slowly. Mix well. Scrape into 9 inch buttered round cake pan. Pat into an even layer. Prick the surface of the dough all over with a fork. Bake at 325 degrees for 30 minutes. Break apart for servings.

LAZY DAY CHOCOLATE CHERRY BARS

2 eggs, beaten

1 box chocolate cake mix

1 (16 ounce) can cherry pie filling

1 teaspoon almond extract

Place all ingredients in a bowl. Mix well. Pour into a 15½ x 10½ x 1 inch greased pan. Bake at 350 degrees for 30 minutes. Cool and frost.

ROCKY SNAPPERS

2 (8 ounce) bars milk chocolate

2½ cups miniature marshmallows

1 cup chopped nuts

Line an 8 x 8 inch baking pan with foil, butter and set aside. In top of a double boiler, melt chocolate, stirring constantly. Remove from heat immediately after chocolate melts, to avoid sugaring. Add marshmallows and nuts. Stir to coat. Spread in prepared pan. Chill to harden. Break into bite size pieces for serving. Makes 36.

LIZ HOLTZMAN became the youngest woman ever elected to Congress in 1972 at age 31. She defeated an opponent who had been in office for 50 years. Because she had little money to spend, she campaigned outside Brooklyn movie theatres where thousands were lined up to see The Godfather.

CAPTAIN KRUNCH® COOKIES

1 (24 ounce) package almond bark

1 cup peanut butter

8 cups Captain Krunch® cereal

1 cup salted peanuts

Melt almond bark according to package directions. Add peanut butter and mix. Remove from heat and stir in cereal and peanuts. Drop by spoonfuls onto waxed paper. Cool.

CUCKOO'S BITS

2 (6 ounce) milk chocolate bars

2 cups Cheerios®

2 cups Kix® cereal

Melt chocolate over hot water. Cool. Gently stir in cereal until well coated. Drop with tablespoon onto wax paper. Place in refrigerator until set. Makes 3 dozen.

CHOCOLATE CRUNCH BAR

1 (6 ounce) bar semisweet chocolate, chopped

1 (6 ounce) bar white chocolate, chopped

1 cup frosted rice cereal

Place semisweet chocolate and white chocolate in separate glass bowls. Microwave 2 minutes on high. Stir ½ cup of the cereal into each bowl. Alternately spoon mixture side by side onto sprayed cookie sheet. Swirl together with a knife to marble slightly. Refrigerate until firm enough to break into pieces. Makes ¾ pound.

VINNIE REAM HOXIE was the first woman to receive a U.S. government commission for sculpture (at age 15 or 18—sources disagree). Her full length statue of Abraham Lincoln, unveiled in 1871, still stands in the Capitol Rotunda. It was based on a bust she had modeled from life shortly before his assassination. She was born in Wisconsin, studied in Washington and Paris, and did portraits of Ulysses S. Grant and Horace Greeley.

PUMPKIN CRUNCH

2 (8 ounce) cans pumpkin pie filling

1 box spice cake mix

1 cup chopped pecans

2 sticks butter or margarine, melted

In greased and floured 13 x 9 inch pan, pour pumpkin pie filling. Sprinkle spice cake mix evenly over top. Sprinkle chopped nuts over spice cake. Pour butter over mixture. Bake at 325 degrees for 70 to 75 minutes.

M & M'S® KRISPIES SQUARES

¼ cup margarine

1 (10 ounce) package marshmallows

1 cup M & M's®

5 cups rice cereal

Melt margarine over low heat. Add marshmallows and stir until melted. Remove from heat and add cereal and M & M's®. Stir until well coated. Pour and press mixture evenly into buttered 13 x 9 inch pan. Cool. Cut into squares.

QUICK FIX TREAT

8 graham cracker rectangles

2 (⅛ ounce) milk chocolate candy bars

4 marshmallows

Top 4 graham crackers with ½ candy bar and 1 marshmallow. Cover with remaining graham crackers. Wrap individually in napkin or paper towel. Arrange cookies on plate. Microwave on high level for 2 minutes. Let stand 2 minutes. Makes 4 servings.

FLORENCE GRIFFITH JOYNER

(Flo-Jo) won four gold medals and captured the attention of the world with her long hair, one-legged running outfits and brightly painted fingernails at the 1988 Seoul Olympic games. She broke world records in the 100 and 200 meter events. She was later appointed as co-chair of the President's Council on Physical Fitness and Sports.

BUTTER SCOTCH KRISPIE TREATS

1 (6 ounce) package butterscotch pieces

3 tablespoons butter or margarine

3 cups miniature marshmallows

3 cups rice cereal

Place butterscotch pieces and butter in a 2 quart glass casserole. Microwave uncovered on high level until melted, about 3 minutes. Add marsh-mallows and microwave until melted. Blend un-til smooth. Stir rice cereal into marshmallow mixture. Press into casserole. Cool and cut into squares. Makes 16 squares.

PECAN SNACK

1 pound pecans

2 tablespoons butter

1 teaspoon cinnamon

½ cup sugar

Put pecans in saucepan and add butter and cin-namon. Heat on low. Stir pecans 3 minutes. Pour onto cookie sheets and sprinkle with sugar. Cool.

TING-A-LINGS

2 (6 ounce) packages semisweet
   chocolate chips

1 cup Spanish peanuts

2 cups chow mein noodles

Melt chocolate over low heat. Gently stir in peanuts and noodles. Drop with tablespoons onto wax paper. Place in refrigerator until chocolate is set.

BARBARA JORDAN *was the first woman and first black person to enter Boston University Law School. The first black woman elected to the Texas State Senate. The first black woman to be elected from a Southern state to Congress. The first black woman to be the main speaker at a national party convention—the Democratic National Convention in 1976.*

COW PIES

2 cups of chocolate chips

1 tablespoon of milk

½ cup raisins

½ cup chopped slivered almonds

Over low heat, melt chocolate chips in milk, stirring until smooth. Remove from heat; stirring in raisins and almonds. Drop by tablespoon onto wax paper. Chill. Makes 2 dozen.

MICROWAVE POPCORN BALLS

¼ cup margarine

1 (10½ ounce) bag miniature marshmallows

1 (4 serving) box flavored gelatin

12 cups popped popcorn

Combine margarine and marshmallows in large microwave safe bowl. Microwave on high for 2 minutes or until marshmallows are puffed. Add gelatin and stir until well blended. Pour marshmallow mixture over popped popcorn. Stir to coat well. Shape into balls with buttered hands. Makes 2 dozen.

HELEN KELLER, *blind and deaf from her second year in life, epitomized the triumph of an indomitable spirit over incredibly restricting physical handicaps. She graduated with honors from Radcliffe College and dedicated her life's work to promoting the cause of the blind and deaf-blind.*

CARAMEL POPCORN BALLS

1 cup caramel chips

1 tablespoon butter

2 tablespoons milk

5 cups popped popcorn

Combine chips and butter in a saucepan. Melt over low heat, stirring constantly. Add milk and stir until smooth. Remove from heat. Add popcorn and mix lightly until well coated with the caramel mixture. Form into balls using ¼ cup mixture for each. Cool. Makes 12 balls.

HONEY CRUNCH POPCORN

12 cups popped popcorn

½ cup chopped pecans

½ cup packed brown sugar

½ cup honey

Combine popcorn and pecans in large bowl. Mix lightly. Set aside and combine brown sugar and honey in saucepan. Cook over medium heat until it comes to a boil. Pour over popcorn. Toss to coat evenly. Spray cookie sheet with cooking spray. Spread popcorn onto sheet. Bake at 300 degrees for 30 minutes. Stir after 15 minutes.

ANNE SULLIVAN MACY was blinded by trachoma at age five, then had her sight restored by several operations when she was fourteen. She became Helen Keller's teacher at the age of 20, and devoted her life to her pupil. Their story is immortalized in the play and motion picture, The Miracle Worker.

QUICK FIX CUSTARD

2 cups milk

2 eggs

½ cup sugar

½ teaspoon vanilla

Place milk, eggs, sugar, and vanilla in a quart bowl. Mix until well blended. Pour into 5 custard cups. Sprinkle with nutmeg. Set cups in cold water in a pan with a tight fitting lid. Bring to a boil. Turn off heat and let set with cover on for 45 minutes.

BAKED CUSTARD

4 eggs, slightly beaten

3½ cups milk

7 tablespoons sugar

2 teaspoons vanilla

Combine ingredients and mix well. Pour into 8 custard cups. Set cups in shallow baking pan and add 1 inch hot water to pan. Bake at 350 degrees for 40 to 45 minutes. Chill. Makes 8 servings.

CREAMY CUSTARD

3 cups milk, scalded

1 cup sugar

4 eggs, beaten

1 cup whipping cream

In a saucepan, heat milk to scalding point. Remove from heat. Stir in sugar and eggs and add cream. Return to heat and cook. Stirring constantly until the mixture thickens. Makes 4 servings.

FLORENCE NIGHTINGALE (1820-1902) was the daughter of a wealthy family who spurned marriage to establish the nobility of the nursing profession. By shifting the emphasis in medical treatment from corrective care to preventative measures, she saved untold numbers of lives. The founder of modern secular nursing, she instituted revolutionary reforms in public health and hospital management.

FRUIT JUICE TAPIOCA

2½ cups pineapple juice

4 tablespoons quick cooking tapioca

Pinch of cinnamon

Combine all ingredients in saucepan. Wait 5 minutes. Then cook and stir over low heat until mixture boils. Remove from heat and cover. Wait 30 minutes and then stir well. Spoon into 6 dessert cups and chill. Makes 6 servings.

OLD FASHIONED RICE PUDDING

2 cups rice

2 cups raisins

2 cups sugar

2 quarts milk

In saucepan, add all ingredients. Cook on low heat for 30 minutes. Cool.

SHAKER RICE PUDDING

½ cup sugar

1 quart milk

¼ cup uncooked rice

1 teaspoon cinnamon

Mix all ingredients together and put in baking dish. Bake at 250 degrees for 4 hours. Stir occasionally during first 2 hours, then do not touch. Serve with cream. Makes 2 to 3 servings.

When **FRANCES PERKINS** *was appointed by President Franklin Roosevelt to be Secretary of Labor in 1933 she became the first woman to hold a cabinet post in the United States. Her tenure lasted throughout the Roosevelt administration, making her the second-longest-serving cabinet member in U.S. history.*

FAST AND EASY RICE PUDDING

2 cups water

½ teaspoon salt

½ cup rice

1 (4 serving) box cook and serve
    vanilla pudding

Boil water and salt together. Add rice. Cook until done. Fix vanilla pudding according to package directions. Add to rice. Mix and cool.

GENE'S FRIED APPLES

2 tablespoons margarine

6 – 8 apples, peeled

¾ cup sugar

1 teaspoon cinnamon

Melt margarine in skillet. Slice apples and put in skillet. Cover and cook until half done (10 minutes). Add sugar and stir. Cover and cook until desired consistency. Stir in cinnamon and cook for two to three minutes. Makes 4 to 6 servings.

NO-GUILT BANANA SPLIT

1 small banana

½ cup vanilla yogurt

¼ cup halved seedless grapes

¼ cup sliced strawberries

Peel and split banana lengthwise. Place in sundae dish. Top with yogurt, grapes, and strawberries. Makes 1 serving.

The daughter of Italian immigrant parents, **GERALDINE FERRARO,** *became the first woman to be nominated for vice president by a major political party in the United States. Her work with the Democratic Platform Committee persuaded Walter Mondale to pick her as his running mate. They lost the 1984 election to the Republican incumbents.*

BANANAS IN CARAMEL SAUCE

4 tablespoons brown sugar

2 tablespoons butter

4 medium ripe bananas, peeled and left whole

Put brown sugar and butter in baking dish and microwave on high for 2 minutes. Add bananas and spoon the sauce over to coat well. Microwave on high for 1 minute. Serve with vanilla ice cream or cookies.

CHERRY DELIGHT

1 (20 ounce) can cherry pie filling

1 (6 ounce) can crushed pineapple

1 (14 ounce) can sweetened condensed milk

2 cups frozen whipped topping

Mix all ingredients together and chill. Makes 6 servings.

PEACHES AND CREAM

3 cups sliced fresh peaches

1 cup sour cream

2 tablespoons sugar

¼ teaspoon grated lemon rind

Place sliced peaches in 6 sherbet glasses. Combine remaining ingredients and spoon over peaches.

EDNA FERBER won a Pulitzer Prize for her 1924 novel, "So Big," which deals with a widow trying to support herself and her son. Many of her stories became popular movies: "Cimarron," 1930, the story of the 1889 Oklahoma land run, "Showboat" and "Giant." She started as a short story writer and wrote several popular plays with George S. Kaufman, such as "Dinner at Eight" and "Stage Door."

SUMMERTIME PEACH PUDDING

1 (4 serving) box peach-flavored gelatin

½ cup hot milk

1½ cups cold milk

1 (4 serving) box instant vanilla pudding

In a bowl, dissolve gelatin in hot milk and set aside. Meanwhile, in a mixing bowl, beat cold milk and pudding mix on low speed for 2 minutes. Add gelatin mixture. Mix well. Let stand 5 minutes. Spoon into individual dishes. Garnish with peaches and whipped topping. Makes 4 servings.

PUDDING IN A CLOUD

2 cups frozen whipped topping

2 cups milk

1 (4 serving) box instant chocolate pudding

Spoon whipped topping evenly into 6 dessert dishes using back of spoon. Spread whipped topping onto bottom and up the side of each dish. Pour milk into medium bowl. Add pudding mix. Beat for 2 minutes. Spoon pudding into center of whipped topping. Refrigerate until ready to serve. Makes 6 servings.

A southern belle, who married a wealthy English playboy, **JULIETTE GORDON LOW,** *at age 52 channeled the organizational and social skills that had made her a world famous hostess into another direction. She founded the Girl Scouts of America, where millions of girls acquire basic survival skills and enjoy meeting and making friends with girls of diverse social and cultural backgrounds.*

EVE'S PINEAPPLE CREAM

1 (13½ ounce) can crushed pineapple, undrained

½ pound marshmallows (22 to 30), chopped

1 cup whipping cream, whipped

In saucepan heat pineapple, add marshmallows and stir untilk dissolved. Remove from heat and cool. When partially set, fold in whipped cream. Chill 2 hours (or overnight). Makes 8 servings.

STRAWBERRY ANGEL DESSERT

1 (4 serving) box strawberry-flavored gelatin

1 (8 ounce) package frozen strawberries

1 (8 ounce) tub frozen whipped topping, softened

½ of angel food cake, torn into pieces

Mix gelatin as directed on box. Add frozen strawberries and mix. Place in refrigerator until it begins to set. Add whipped topping and then cake. Mix lightly and pour into a casserole dish. Put in refrigerator until set.

In 1915 **GEORGIA O'KEEFE** *sent some of her drawings to a friend with the understanding that he not show them to anyone else. When she found out they were being exhibited in a New York gallery, she demanded they be removed—but she was persuaded to let them remain. She is best known for her dramatic paintings of sun bleached desert bones; most of her later work was painted in Taos, New Mexico. She is the most famous woman artist of our times.*

DOESN'T LAST DESSERT

12 ice cream sandwiches

1 (8 ounce) tub frozen whipped topping

2 large Butterfinger® candy bars, crushed

Line the bottom of a 12 x 9 baking dish with ice cream sandwiches. Spread whipped topping thickly and evenly over sandwiches. Sprinkle Butterfinger® crumbs over top. Cover and freeze until ready to serve. Makes 8 servings.

FRUIT JUICE POPSICLES

1½ cups white grape juice

1½ cups red grape juice

1 tablespoon lemon juice

1 tablespoon sugar

Combine all ingredients and pour into popsicle molds. Insert popsicle sticks and freeze until firm. Makes 6 servings.

WATERMELON SHERBET

1 quart watermelon pulp

⅓ cup sugar

2 tablespoons lime juice

Put watermelon pulp in blender and puree. Dissolve sugar in lime juice. Combine watermelon and sugar-lime mixture. Place in ice cream freezer and follow operating instructions. Makes 1 quart.

BILLIE JEAN KING won $100,000, the largest purse ever paid for a single tennis match at that time, when she defeated tennis pro Bobby Riggs in three straight sets at the Houston Astrodome in 1973. The "Battle of the Sexes" drew a combined live and television audience of 60 million people. She went on to win six Wimbledon and four U.S. Open singles titles.

LITE CHOCOLATE ICE CREAM

½ gallon low fat chocolate milk

2 (8 ounce) tubs lite frozen whipped topping

1 (12 ounce) can low fat condensed milk

Mix chocolate milk, whipped topping, and condensed milk. Freeze according to ice cream freezer directions. Makes 4 servings.

PINEAPPLE ICE CREAM

1 cup sour cream

1 (14 ounce) can sweetened condensed milk

2 cups milk

1¼ cups crushed pineapple

Combine sour cream and sweetened condensed milk; add milk. Freeze in 2-quart ice cream freezer, using 6 parts ice to 1 part salt, till partially frozen. Add pineapple, freeze firm. Remove dasher. Cover top freezer can with several sheets of waxed paper; replace lid. Pack in ice and salt. Allow to ripen 1 hour. Makes 2 quarts.

SWEET BITE ICE CREAM

1 pint vanilla ice cream

2 tablespoons finely chopped crystallized ginger

½ teaspoon cinnamon

In a large bowl, beat ice cream, ginger, and cinnamon until blended. Return to carton and freeze until ready to use. Makes 2 to 3 servings.

SAPPHO (c.650-580 BC), Greek lyric poet, was called the "tenth muse" by Plato, and is considered the greatest woman poet of antiquity. Her poems are on themes of love and personal relationships, often with other women. She was born on the island of Lesbos, and her name today is often associated with female homosexuality. Only two complete poems of hers exist today, but many fragments have been found in Egypt.

BUTTERSCOTCH SAUCE

1 cup miniature marshmallows

1 cup butterscotch flavored pieces

¼ cup milk

In saucepan, add marshmallows, butterscotch, and milk. Heat on low, stirring constantly until smooth. Serve warm over ice cream. Makes 1½ cups.

CARAMEL SAUCE

28 caramel candies

¼ cup half and half or milk

⅛ teaspoon vanilla

Combine all ingredients in a small bowl. Microwave on high for 2 to 4 minutes. Stir after each minute.

HOT FUDGE SAUCE

1 cup chocolate chips

¼ cup marshmallow cream

¼ cup milk

ELIZABETH ARDEN, a Canadian, became the first major figure in the American cosmetics industry. She opened her first beauty salon in New York City in 1910.

Combine all ingredients in a bowl, microwave on medium for 2 to 3 minutes. Stirring once during cooking time. Serve sauce warm or cold. Makes 1 cup.

ORANGE SAUCE

¾ cup sugar

2 teaspoons grated orange peel

1 cup orange juice

Mix all ingredients together in saucepan. Cook until thick and clear, stirring constantly. Makes 1¼ cups.

PRALINE PARFAIT SAUCE

⅓ cup water

⅓ cup packed brown sugar

1 cup light corn syrup

1 cup chopped pecans

Bring the water to a boil. Add sugar, corn syrup and pecans. Cook slowly until mixture comes to a boil. Pour into a container and refrigerate. Mixture will thicken when cooled. Pour over ice cream.

COCOA WHIPPED CREAM

1 cup chilled whipping cream

¼ cup confectioners' sugar

2 tablespoons cocoa

½ teaspoon vanilla

Beat cream, sugar, cocoa and vanilla. Chill. Makes 2 quarts.

JOY ADAMSON *was an Austrian-born British naturalist and writer. She and her husband, game warden George Adamson, lived in Kenya where she studied and painted wildlife. She made her name with a series of books about the lioness Elsa:* Born Free, Elsa, Forever Free, *and* Elsa and Her Cubs. *She was murdered in her home by tribesmen*

RUM-FLAVORED WHIPPED CREAM

2 cups chilled whipping cream

½ cup confectioners' sugar

2 teaspoons rum flavoring

In a chilled bowl add cream, confectioners' sugar, and rum flavoring. Beat until stiff.

in 1980.
JULIE ANDREWS, *an English singer and actress was from a show business family. She starred on Broadway in* The Boyfriend *in 1954,* My Fair Lady *in 1956, and* Camelot *in 1960. She won an Oscar for her film debut in* Mary Poppins *in 1964, was nominated for* Sound of Music, *and was voted the world's most popular star. To get away from her prim image she played a breast-baring movie star in* S.O.B. *and a transvestite in* Victor/Victoria.

CHOCOLATE-DIPPED STRAWBERRIES

½ pound sweet chocolate

1 tablespoon shortening

1 quart strawberries, washed

Combine chocolate and shortening. Microwave on medium for 3 to 4 minutes, or until chocolate is melted. Dip strawberries in chocolate one at a time; place onto wax paper. Chill. Makes 6 servings.

COCONUT BONBONS

1 (3 ounce) package cream cheese, softened

2½ cups sifted confectioners' sugar

¼ teaspoon vanilla extract

1 (3½ ounce) can flaked coconut

Beat cream cheese until light and fluffy. Add sugar gradually and continue beating until well mixed. Add vanilla and mix well. Form into bite-size balls. Roll balls in coconut. Chill for several hours. Makes 40.

COCONUT CARAMELS

3 cups packed brown sugar

1 cup milk

1 teaspoon butter

1 cup flaked coconut

Melt 1 cup brown sugar, add milk and remaining sugar and butter. Boil to soft ball. Add coconut, beat and drop by teaspoonfuls onto wax paper. Cool.

CARAMEL CLUSTERS

1 (14 ounce) package caramels

¼ cup half and half

5 cups rice cereal

Place caramels in a large saucepan. Add half and half. Cook and stir over low heat until carmels melt. Remove from heat and stir in rice cereal. Drop by tablespoons onto waxed paper, let cool. Makes 2½ dozen.

ALMOND BARK CANDY

1 pound white chocolate

1 cup raisins

1 cup whole almonds

Break chocolate into small pieces and place in a 2 quart glass mixing bowl. Microwave, uncovered on high level until chocolate melts, about 5 minutes. Stir in raisins and almonds. Immediately pour a thin layer mixture mixture onto wax paper. Cool. Break into pieces. Makes 1½ pounds.

BARBARA HAMILTON CARTLAND, *the step-grandmother of Princess Diana, published her first novel, Jigsaw, in 1923. She has since produced over 400 best-selling books, mostly romance novels designed for women readers, but also wrote biographies and books on food, health and beauty. She is in the* Guinness Book of Records *for writing 26 books in 1983.*

TAFFY

1 cup sugar

½ cup honey

⅛ teaspoon salt

1 tablespoon butter

Put all ingredients in saucepan. Cook over medium heat until a ball is formed when dropped in cold water. Pour on buttered platter. Cool enough to pull. Butter hands and pull until hard.

HARD TIME CANDY

2 cups sugar

1 cup water

½ cup corn syrup

½ teaspoon of flavoring

Mix the sugar, water, and corn syrup. Boil on high until mixture is ready to burn. Reduce heat. Add flavoring and stir. Pour onto buttered platter. Cut into pieces with scissors. Toss lightly with confectioners' sugar.

CINNAMON CANDY

2¾ cups sugar

¾ cup light corn syrup

¾ cup water

1 teaspoon cinnamon oil

In saucepan, add sugar, syrup and water. Cook over medium heat and bring to a hard boil, about 7 minutes. Remove from heat, add cinnamon oil, and pour over buttered cookie sheet. Let cool, then break up. Can add a few drops of red food coloring.

RACHEL CARSON, *an American author and marine biologist made "ecology" a household word, and sparked an environmental revolution. In her 1962 book,* Silent Spring, *she warned that indiscriminate use of pesticides threatened all life on the planet. It led to the banning of such chemicals as DDT. Some of the most beautifully written works of natural history ever published are her* Edge of the Sea, *and* The Sea Around Us.

CELEBRATION MINTS

5 tablespoons butter, melted

2½ tablespoons evaporated milk

1 tablespoon mint extract

2 cups confectioners' sugar

Melt butter; add milk, extract, and sugar. Mix in slowly. Knead the mixture and press into rubber molds (can use food coloring). Makes 60 mints.

BUTTERSCOTCH PEANUT CLUSTERS

1 (6 ounce) package butterscotch pieces

½ cup peanut butter

1½ cups whole salted peanuts

Melt butterscotch pieces and peanut butter in top of double boiler over hot water. Add nuts. Stir until well blended. Drop by teaspoonful onto wax paper. Chill until firm. Makes 3 dozen.

CRÈME FUDGE DROPS

2 (16 ounce) bags old fashioned cream drops

2 tablespoons margarine

2 teaspoons vanilla

1 cup pecans, chopped

Put cream drops in a large microwave safe dish. Microwave 2½ minutes on high. Stir the mixture. Stir in margarine and vanilla. Microwave for 2 minutes on high. Add pecans. Pour into buttered 11 x 7 inch dish. Cool before cutting. Makes 2½ pounds.

MARY BAKER EDDY (1821-1910), the founder of the Christian Science religion suffered a variety of illnesses in her first 45 years. In her Bible she read Matthew 9:1-8 about a man cured of palsy. She rose from her bed and walked. Mary's study convinced her that her own mind had joined with the mind of God to insure her recovery. Her writings and teachings led her to found the Church of Christ Scientist, located today all over North America and Western Europe. She also founded the newspaper, the Christian Science Monitor.

TAYLOR CALDWELL
was the author of 38 internationally best selling novels. Before her death, in 1985, she had sold over 30 million copies. The subjects of her novels fall into three main categories: tough and ruthless men; historical figures enmeshed in an invented world; and the hidden life of biblical characters. Testimony of Two Men *and* Captains and the Kings *were serialized for television. Some of the writing awards she received were a Gold Medal from the National League of American Penswomen (1948) and the DAR National Award in 1956.*

CRUNCHY FUDGE DROPS

1 (12 ounce) package semisweet chocolate chips

¼ cup margarine

3½ cups granola without raisins

½ cup chopped dried fruit

Melt chocolate and margarine in saucepan over low heat, stirring frequently until smooth. Stir in cereal and dried fruit. Drop by heaping teaspoonfuls onto a waxed paper lined cookie sheet. Chill until set. Makes 5 dozen.

SNICKERS BAR FUDGE

1 (12 ounce) package semisweet chocolate chips

1 (15.6 ounce) can creamy milk chocolate frosting

2 (3.7 ounce) Snickers candy bars, chopped

Line an 8 inch square pan with foil, extending foil over edges. Spray lightly with nonstick cooking spray. Set aside. Melt chips in medium saucepan over low heat, stirring constantly. Remove from heat. Reserve 2 tablespoons of the candy bars. Add frosting and remaining candy bars. Blend well. Spread in foil-lined pan. Sprinkle with reserved candy bars. Refrigerate 1 hour or until firm.

TOFFEE FUDGE

¾ cup packed brown sugar

½ cup butter

1 cup chopped pecans

½ cup semisweet chocolate chips

Grease a 9 inch square pan. Spread pecans over bottom of pan. In saucepan slowly boil brown sugar and butter for 7 minutes. Stirring constantly. Remove from heat and spread over nuts immediately. Sprinkle chocolate over hot mixture. Cover pan so heat will melt chocolate. Spread chocolate evenly over candy. Cut into squares while hot. Refrigerate to set the chocolate. Makes 36 1½ inch pieces.

CHOCOLATE CHIP FUDGE

1 (14 ounce) can sweetened condensed milk

1 (12 ounce) package semisweet chocolate chips

1 teaspoon vanilla

1½ cups chopped nuts

Heat milk and chocolate chips in 2 quart saucepan over low heat, stirring constantly until chocolate is melted and mixture is smooth. Remove from heat, stir in vanilla and nuts. Spread mixture evenly in pan. Refrigerate until firm. Cut into 1¼ inch squares. Makes 3 dozen.

AIMEE SIMPLE McPHERSON *was flamboyant and imaginative and was hugely successful as an evangelist. In 1918 she founded the Foursquare Gospel Movement in Los Angeles. For nearly two decades she preached and healed in the $1.5 million Angelus Temple in L.A. She had her own radio station, Bible school, and magazine. She was often the center of controversy with several legal suits against her. In 1926, she had a mysterious and unexplained five week disappearance (she claimed to have been kidnapped). It was even questioned whether her death was from a heart attack or an overdose of barbiturates.*

HAZELNUT FUDGE

²/₃ cup evaporated milk

1¾ cups sugar

½ cup halved hazelnuts

2 cups semisweet chocolate chips

Generously grease an 8 inch square cake pan. Combine milk and sugar in saucepan. Bring to a boil over medium heat, stirring constantly. Simmer gently for about 5 minutes. Add hazelnuts and chocolate chips. Stir until the chocolate has melted. Pour into pan and cool. Makes 16 squares.

MOCK PEANUT BRITTLE

1 cup sugar

1 cup corn syrup

1 cup peanut butter

6½ cups corn flakes

Combine sugar and syrup in saucepan. Bring to a boil. Stir in peanut butter until it melts. Pour over corn flakes until all are coated. Spread onto waxed paper to cool.

EASY DO PRALINES

1 (16 ounce) box brown sugar

1 cup whipping cream

3 cups chopped pecans

Mix brown sugar and cream. Mix well. Put into saucepan and cook over medium heat to soft ball stage. Stir in pecans and cook 3 minutes more. Drop by teaspoon onto waxed paper. Let cool. Makes 1½ cups.

MARILYN MONROE *became the ultimate sex symbol of motion pictures. Her first claim to fame was a nude calendar pose. She starred in many movies as the "sexy dumb blonde,"* such as How to Marry a Millionaire *and* Gentlemen Prefer Blondes. *She was married to playwright Arthur Miller and to baseball great, Joe DiMaggio (who kept flowers on her grave until his death). Much controversy centered on her relationship with President John F. Kennedy (and her sultry happy birthday song to him) and his brother, Attorney General Robert Kennedy.*

QUICK AND EASY PRALINES

1 cup sugar

1 cup packed dark brown sugar

1½ cups whipping cream

2 cups chopped pecans

In a pan over low heat, dissolve sugar, brown sugar, and cream. Cook at a low boil, stirring often, until mixture forms soft ball. Cool slightly. Beat mixture until it starts to thicken. Add pecans. Drop batter from teaspoon onto waxed paper to form individual pralines. Cool. Makes 1½ pounds.

CREAMY CARAMELS DELIGHT

1 (7 ounce) box fudge frosting mix

½ cup butter

½ cup whipping cream

1 cup light corn syrup

Put fudge frosting into large saucepan and add butter, cream, and corn syrup. Cook over medium heat to 250 degrees or hard ball stage. Pour into buttered 9 inch square pan. Let cool. Makes 1½ pounds.

BARBRA STREISAND *began singing in amateur contests in New York and had Broadway successes in* I Can Get It For You Wholesale *in 1963 and* Funny Girl *in 1964— which she repeated on screen in her film debut in 1968 and won an Academy Award. Her television special, "My Name Is Barbra," won five Emmy Awards, and she has won numerous Grammy Awards including three as best female vocalist (1964–65 and 1978). She has extended her talents and produces and directs motion pictures.*

index

NOTES

OTHER COOKBOOKS AVAILABLE FROM CREATIVE IDEAS PUBLISHING

To order, fill out enclosed order form or call 1-800-673-0768 and on the web at www.busywomanscookbook.com.

BUSY WOMAN'S COOKBOOK A national bestseller by Sharon and Gene McFall. Over 350,000 copies sold. It has over 500 mouth-watering 3 and 4 ingredient recipes and more than 200 short stories and facts about famous and influential women. $18.95

BUSY WOMAN'S SLOW COOKER COOKBOOK by Sharon and Gene McFall and Linda Burgett. Over 500 delicious slow cooker recipes with few ingredients (all common or easily found) and 250 stories and facts about famous and influential women. $18.95

COOKIN' WITH WILL ROGERS by Sharon and Gene McFall. Has over 560 delicious country cookin' recipes with over 100 Will Rogers quotes, 60 pictures and 50 stories of one of America's most beloved humorists. "Only a fool argues with a skunk, a mule or a cook." Will Rogers. $19.95.

GET ME OUT OF THE KITCHEN by Sharon and Gene McFall. 500 easy to prepare recipes. Special low-fat and low-cal recipes as well as helpful cooking hints. A wonderful cookbook. $18.95.

HOME MADE BLESSINGS by Diane Reasoner. Over 400 excellent tasting recipes, straight forward instructions and ingredients that are found in any pantry. Inspirational sayings on every page that will brighten your day. $19.95.

IF I GOTTA COOK MAKE IT QUICK by Shelley Plettl. Over 500 Hassle Free recipes using just a few ingredients. Includes: Easy to Prepare Slow Cooker Recipes; Helpful Hints and Fun Facts; How to Adapt Your Favorite Recipes to the Slow Cooker; How to Substitute One Ingredient for Another; Uses of Herbs and Spices; Basic Rules for Table Manners. $18.95

JUST ENOUGH FOR TWO by Sharon McFall, Linda Burgett and Shelley Plettl. Over 400 great recipes with few ingredients, designed for one or two people, helpful hints and much useful information. A must for singles or couples. $18.95

MILD TO WILD MEXICAN COOKBOOK by Linda Burgett. Over 400 tantalizing recipes from south of the border. Every recipe tells you if it is hot, medium or mild-so you have no big surprises. Also has fun facts on ingredients. One word for this book—Wonderful. $18.95.

Please send _____ copies of_____

@ $18.95 (U.S.) each $_____

Postage and handling @ $3.50 each $_____

TOTAL $_____

Check or Credit Card (Canada-credit card only)

Charge to my ☐ Master Card or Visa Card

account # _____

expiration date _____

signature _____

MAIL TO:
Creative Ideas Publishing
7916 N.W. 23rd St.
P.M.B. 115
Bethany, OK 73008-5135
1-800-673-0768
www.busywomanscookbook.com

Name _____

Address _____

City _____ State _____ Zip _____

Phone (day) _____ (night) _____

ORDER ON THE WEB: www.busywomanscookbook.com

— —

Please send _____ copies of
Busy Woman's Slow Cooker Cookbook

@ $18.95 (U.S.) each $_____

Postage and handling @ $3.50 each $_____

TOTAL $_____

Check or Credit Card (Canada-credit card only)

Charge to my ☐ Master Card or Visa Card

account # _____

expiration date _____

signature _____

MAIL TO:
Creative Ideas Publishing
7916 N.W. 23rd St.
P.M.B. 115
Bethany, OK 73008-5135
1-800-673-0768
www.busywomanscookbook.com

Name _____

Address _____

City _____ State _____ Zip _____

Phone (day) _____ (night) _____

ORDER ON THE WEB: www.busywomanscookbook.com

SHARE YOUR
FAVORITE RECIPE

Do you have a favorite quick and easy recipe? Do family and friends ask you for it? Would you like to see it in a national cookbook?

If so, lease send your favorite quick and easy recipe to us. If we use it in a future cookbook, you will be given credit in the book for the recipe, and will receive a free copy of the book.

*Submit to: Creative Ideas Publishing
PMB 115
7916 N.W. 23rd Street
Bethany, OK 73003-5135*